Daddy's Little Girl

This book is a work of non- fiction based on the life, experiences and recollections of the author. In some cases names, places, dates and the detail of events have been changed to protect the privacy of others.

TONI MAGUIRE

WITH LYNN MURRAY

Daddy's Little Girl

A picture-perfect family with a terrible secret

EBURY
PRESS

1 3 5 7 9 10 8 6 4 2

Ebury Press, an imprint of Ebury Publishing
20 Vauxhall Bridge Road
London SW1V 2SA

Ebury Press is part of the Penguin Random House group of companies whose
addresses can be found at global.penguinrandomhouse.com

Penguin
Random House
UK

Copyright © Toni Maguire and Lynn Murray 2020

Toni Maguire and Lynn Murray have asserted their right to be identified as
the authors of this Work in accordance with the Copyright, Designs and
Patents Act 1988

First published by Ebury Press in 2020

www.penguin.co.uk

A CIP catalogue record for this book is available from the British Library

ISBN 9781529104004

Typeset in 11.25/16 pt Garamond MT Pro
by Integra Software Services Pvt. Ltd, Pondicherry

Printed and bound in Great Britain by Clays Ltd, Elcograf S.p.A.

In loving memory of my brother Andy.
This world was too hard for you. Loved and always and
forever in our hearts.

Contents

Prologue

2014

I thought my life was settled then but that did not stop me wanting to find the root cause of the lingering fear that still disturbed my dreams all these years later. Like most people, I had anxieties I attempted to label as being rational.

My daughter disappearing from my sight for a nanosecond.

The ringing of the phone during the night when someone I love is in hospital.

Or a friend who left me to drive a long distance and has forgotten to let me know of their safe arrival home, despite all their assurances.

Yes, those are the ones I saw as normal.

Then there were the irrational ones, the ones that made me angry with myself. For after all I had achieved, I was still frightened by the dark and the creaks my old house made as it settled down for the night. And should I have been woken by the sound of soft footsteps or the click of the landing light being switched on, even though my rational mind told me it was just my four-year-old daughter seeking the warmth of my bed, my irrational one said something quite different. It was then that the sweat broke out on my forehead and my knuckles turned white as my fingers clutched the duvet tightly for comfort.

One thing I was sure of was that I was not born with that fear. No baby is, not when the world is brand new to them and they have not yet been faced with the cruel reality that fate may hand them. Much as I had tried to force it, my mind refused to take me back to a time before I was four years old, though the memories of what began to happen then were still clear in my head ... unfortunately, all too vividly.

Part One
My Small Self

Chapter One

For almost all of my life I believed my story began the day I was born.

It was not until I reached my forties that I discovered it had started much earlier. The day I learnt about our family's secrets was the day I searched for the photograph albums that, when small, I had watched my mother filling painstakingly with our collective memories.

Had they been thrown out, I wondered, as I frantically went through the boxes my father had brought down from Scotland and left for me to look through.

One by one, I opened them, impatiently tossing out shabby old clothes, a couple of dented saucepans, a few kitchen utensils and, surprisingly, some books by well-known authors I had never seen him read. Just as I was thinking they were not there and becoming resigned to accepting that he had not saved those albums, my fingers touched several firm oblong objects at the very bottom of the box: I had found them.

Blowing off the fine layer of dust, which over time had dulled their shiny red covers, I sat cross-legged on the floor, pulled them onto my knees and started putting them in order.

There were two dating from the three-year period before I was born and ten after that: one for each year before my mother knew that she was going to disappear from our lives. As I examined the images I had not seen for so long, I decided I did not want to leave what appeared to be the only record of my and my brother's early years in those albums' plastic pockets. I guessed there might be some I would want to make disappear and Katy, my inquisitive little daughter, would be certain to ask about the empty spaces I would have created. Instead, I opened each of those pockets and then carefully removed every photograph.

I had an idea, which could make showing them to my daughter easier for me: keep the ones I wanted and turn them into a video. She was still young enough to take delight in us watching it together, but also old enough to have started asking questions about her grandparents. I think she was the only child at school who did not have any. Or rather, any that I had been prepared to let her meet. She needed answers. Using the video, I would be able to tell her stories of all the people she would see on it, although not necessarily totally truthful ones.

Luckily, Katy loved the stories I made up more than the ones in the books I bought her. Ever since I had written about how our cat grew wings, which took her to a magic place called 'Cat Land', she had pestered me for more.

There were two people in the video that Katy had developed close bonds to. A little bit of embellishment would also be needed on their childhoods, I thought ruefully.

Of course, the question 'What are you doing, Mummy?' was asked by her repeatedly. Each time, I answered with a smile, 'You'll just have to wait and see, sweetie.' Not that waiting patiently was something my daughter was good at. But I was determined she would not see it until I had made the sequence of the pictures look as attractive as possible.

I watched them flitting across the screen carefully, but they did not, I realised, give the impression that they were the loving record of my brother's and my childhood. Definitely, for Katy's sake, a little bit of tweaking would have to be done to make it appear so. Still, at her tender young age, hopefully she would not understand that. For what the albums' contents showed was a well-put-together deception. Every photo my mother had chosen to place in them was designed to show unsuspecting eyes images of the perfect family.

A quick click and I was transported back inside the immaculate house I had spent my early years in. There was the lounge, as my mother called it, where cushions were always plumped to perfection, curtains tied back with gold-edged tassels and fresh flowers sat in sparkling crystal vases. The difference between that room and the ones my friends with children have is that not one child's toy marred its polished perfection. But then we were not allowed to play with ours anywhere outside our bedrooms. They might have just made the house look 'lived-in' in my words, or 'untidy' being the sentiments voiced by my parents.

No doubt guests imagined that we had all spent the morning before they arrived frantically tidying up. But they were wrong: that is how our home always appeared.

I pressed forward and watched the pictures of my parents entertaining friends in their landscaped garden. There was my father, showing his public persona: the loving father and devoted husband, standing next to the gleaming fitted barbecue. His charming smile was fixed firmly in place as he threw meat my mother had marinated onto the metal racks. Behind him my mother, wearing high heels and make-up, was pouring various drinks into their visitors' glasses.

That picture brought back a memory of Dad, not a glimmer of a smile on his face, emphatically stating that he did not approve of women wearing trousers, not even if it was an outside lunch party.

'Not in my house,' I am sure he said, for that was an expression I frequently heard him utter throughout my childhood years.

He also told her to make sure that their children looked neat and tidy as well.

'We want them to do us credit, don't we?' he would tell her with a playful wink.

And there we were, all three of us, with neatly combed hair and freshly ironed clothes. Andy and I sitting together as far away from the adults as possible while Gavin hovered near my father, no doubt trying to win his approval by being useful. Not that he ever succeeded in gaining it when there were no visitors. Publicly, of course, Dad would place an arm around his shoulders. Gavin, who yearned for any show of affection, would see it as a genuine reward for being helpful, not that my father was showing what a wonderful stepfather he was.

The opinion I formed, when older – one I still have – was that my mother, Andy and I were his possessions. Like his house and large car, he wanted to keep us looking shiny and bright. For the man my father was back then wished to see not just admiration but envy in his contemporaries' eyes. He knew only too well that this was not an emotion that Gavin, with his clumsy body and lack of charm, was likely to arouse. And Dad, who only wished to own what was perfect, despised him, if for no other reason than that.

I flicked through more images of us, the model family.

There was just one photo of a children's birthday party. I don't know if it was mine or Andy's, nor do I remember who the children were. They would have been the carefully chosen offspring of people my mother wanted as friends. People who disappeared soon after our lives changed.

No point adding that to the video, I decided.

As soon as I pointed the remote at the screen a picture appeared of a pretty blonde woman. Dressed in a cream lacy dress that fell to just below her knees, she was gazing adoringly up at her new husband: my dark-haired, green-eyed and extremely handsome father.

Why, you could see that she was practically incandescent with happiness. I had absolutely no doubt that my mother had been head over heels in love with him then. And what of his feelings? To this day, I don't know. I don't think love was something he was ever really capable of. Possession, yes, but never, I suspected, unconditional love.

In the background I could see an assortment of guests, most with champagne glasses in their hands and benign smiles upon their faces. I'm sure that everyone who was there that day thought what a perfect couple the charming, good-looking and charismatic man and his petite blonde wife made.

Some of them must have known my mother's first husband. Perhaps they had supported her throughout the break-up of what, I have been told, was a disastrous marriage. Just looking at the wedding photographs tells me that her friends and family believed that she had finally found the happiness she deserved.

But did she, I asked myself, deserve happiness? Maybe, but not at the price her children paid for it.

Those well-wishers would also have been happy for the only child from her first marriage, my half-brother Gavin.

He was, I later learnt from my Scottish grandfather, a boy who everyone thought needed a father. 'For what little boy didn't?' my grandfather declared emphatically. 'I mean, mothers are good at cooking and sorting out grazed knees, but a boy needs a father to look up to.' On the day of my parents' wedding he and everyone there believed Gavin had acquired one.

Not wanting to disillusion my grandfather at the time, for he had become an old man when we had that discussion, I stopped myself from saying that all three of us would have been better off if we had a different father to his son.

Let him keep his illusions, I decided. Let him believe, as my mother's friends had, that my father had embraced the seven-year-old boy as though he was his own. The gap my mother's first husband had left was filled and Gavin would have no reason not to stay the happy child he so clearly was on that wedding day.

No doubt everyone who was celebrating my mother's second marriage saw my father as being the perfect role model for his stepson. They must have been aware of how hurt the boy had been, not just by the upheaval of his parents' acrimonious divorce, but his father's complete rejection of him too. For the day that my mother's first husband walked away from the marital home was the last time Gavin ever saw him.

I have never been given an explanation, only that he made it abundantly clear that once his marriage was finished, he had no intention of playing any part in his son's life.

'There is not always an explanation for cruel behaviour,' my English grandmother said when, years later, I questioned her. 'It was most probably that he did not want to be weighed down with any baggage when he and your mother finished. Knowing him, he already had his eyes on her replacement. He was not a kind man.' And those were the only words I ever heard her utter about her first son-in-law.

Chapter Two

As a child I had never thought about the sadness of my half-brother's life, I had just known that he resented both Andy and me. Now, as an adult, I can understand those feelings for I can see clearly the reality of his life with us.

Already he had suffered through the break-up of his parents' marriage. He knew that his father's behaviour was not normal – he had a friend whose parents were separated and every other weekend that boy's father arrived to take him out for the day. Not only that, to compensate for not being there seven days a week, he brought along wonderful presents – toy cars, train sets and Lego, which Gavin was allowed to play with when he visited.

Of course, no matter what was said to him, he hoped his own father would do the same. For weeks, I have learnt, Gavin, forgetting about the rows between his parents and how he was shouted at and pushed aside roughly, would stand by the window, hoping to see his father's car turn into the road. And I can hardly bear to imagine how he felt when that car never appeared.

For the seven-year-old he was then would have felt that it was entirely his fault that his father did not love him.

But on his mother's wedding day, he looked happy.

Involuntarily, my hand clicked on pause. That boy, dressed in a grey jacket with matching trousers, smiling shyly at me through the screen, was a very different boy to the one I had grown up with. I was looking at an appealing child, not the sullen, withdrawn one whom people avoided.

I would, I knew, have liked that boy, but sadly I never got to meet him.

Sitting there, with my finger still on the pause button, I began to really feel the extent of Gavin's sadness during the years he lived with us. On the day of the wedding he was starting to feel secure. His mother, he believed, would always adore him and his new father had given him every indication that he would treat him as a much-loved son.

I felt tears well up when I thought he was completely unaware then of just how his life was really going to be.

It was not until I had watched the end of the section when my parents, all smiles and waves, were climbing into the large American limousine that something dawned on me: where were the photos of their earlier lives, my grandparents, my father as a young man and my mother's early years before she met him? And surely, even if she had ripped up all the ones of her first husband, there must be some of her and Gavin?

It was as though they were stating nothing that had happened before their wedding was of any importance. But then, I asked myself, just what had my mother thought really mattered? For not only were there no photos of her and her first child, but also missing were any baby pictures of either me or my older brother, Andy.

Even though the whole process of buying and developing films was very different forty years ago, I would still have thought that she would have wanted to record as many moments of her children's early years as possible. I certainly had. The moment I saw what resembled a small wriggling tadpole appear on my first scan, I was hopelessly enthralled. I smiled when I thought of all the friends I had shown that one to. On my dressing table is the first picture of Katy, taken when she was placed in my arms after her birth. I can't even count how many shots I took in those early years. There were those first steps, her gummy smile when she was told about the tooth fairy, and then, all too suddenly, it was her first day at school. The list is endless!

So, where were the photos of us? Hadn't my mother wanted to catch her children's first toddling steps, their wide happy smiles when they blew out the candles on their birthday cakes, unwrapped Christmas presents, built snowmen in winter and sandcastles in summer? The answer was of course staring me in the face. Not by what I could see, but what I couldn't.

I felt a wave of tiredness at the lack of them. I had to admit to myself I had hoped there would be enough captured on those strips of plastic film to jog my memory. That somehow, just looking at them would take me back to my childhood. I wanted to understand what went so wrong in our lives. And I needed to piece together not just my parents' earlier lives but mine and Andy's as well.

'Oh, stop being pathetic, Lynn!' I told myself crossly. 'You're just searching for reassurance that you were loved. That's why you're hoping to see loads of pictures showing how you went from baby bump to a leggy twelve-year-old. So, get a grip and get over it, there aren't any. Anyhow, you are making this for your daughter, aren't you, not for yourself. So, let's have a look at those holidays in Scotland. At least then you can show Katy what her great-grandparents were like.'

Yup, I thought, she would definitely love looking at the gypsy caravan. I'll just have to make up some good stories about that. Bring over those Irish leprechauns and have them travelling across the water until they found their home with the gypsies.

And quickly I clicked onto the section of the video showing our Scottish holidays. There were a couple of photos of Andy, but only one with all three of us in it.

Smile, we had been told, and smile we all did. And a happy trio was fixed in time.

Well, that section has been well doctored, I thought wryly.

My mother, in her efforts to convince friends that she had a luxurious lifestyle, was photographed posed outside smart hotels, hoping they would believe that was where we had all stayed. However, the reality was that we had spent those holidays in my grandparents' caravan, parked in the field next to their house.

'I remembered her face screwed up in distaste as she complained incessantly about the outside lavatory and lack of running hot water. It was little more than a slum, she said. But Andy and I loved both the caravan and our grandparents' cottage, with its wood-burning stove. Thinking of that, I can almost smell the wood smoke and the aroma of fresh bread being baked while a stew, thick with homegrown vegetables, simmered away in the pot.

I wish there were some photographs of my grandparents. Although I can remember my grandfather clearly, when I try to picture my grandmother, I have only vague memories of her for although her husband had travelled down to visit us, she never did.

I suppose she knew my mother disapproved of both her and my parents' lifestyle and had not wanted to visit the house they were both so evidently proud of.

All I can conjure up is a vague impression of a plump, white-haired woman who, sitting by the fire, read us stories from beautifully illustrated children's books. I remember her telling us, with a fond smile, 'These are the ones I used to read to your dad when he was just a wee bairn.'

Somehow, I have never been able to imagine my father being a small child.

I do remember more clearly though the picnics she and my grandfather took us children on. Unlike my parents, they treated Gavin as though he was their own grandchild.

If we went to an ice-cream shop, he being the eldest was asked first which flavour he would like. He was encouraged by them to voice his opinion on all manner of things and was listened to as though they felt his view was important.

Whereas Andy and I were called 'bonnie bairns' he was referred to as a 'young man'. I think now they saw his sullenness as being a combination of shyness and insecurity, no doubt caused by going from only child to one of three. They certainly did their best to try to build his confidence. I am pretty certain though they had no idea what was really the reason behind it. And if they had thought the fault lay at our parents' door, it would have been my mother who would have been blamed, for their son could do no wrong in their eyes.

Not being used to either kind words or an adult showing any interest in his opinions, at first Gavin viewed them with suspicion. It took more than a day or two for it to sink in that their affection for him was genuine. When it did, he became noticeably more relaxed. And once again the smile of his from the wedding photos was seen, a smile that disappeared within minutes of us leaving to go home.

Looking back, with a fond smile forming on my lips, at my enjoyment of the simplicity of those holidays, I jostled another memory out of my subconscious mind.

As though it had happened just yesterday, I could see my grandfather with his wide smile and pockets full of sweets, clicking away on his camera.

'I'll send them to you,' he promised and I had waited expectantly for the photos to arrive but to my disappointment they never had.

Or had they? I wondered, as another memory nudged its way in. I was coming out of the kitchen and my mother, oblivious to my presence, was opening a letter that had just arrived. I watched as she flicked through its contents before, with a dismissive snort, placing everything back in the envelope.

Catching sight of me, she just said, 'Oh, only a letter from your grandparents for your father.' No mention was made of the photos and I never asked. But they must have been in the envelope; it was too thick to have contained only a letter.

Think, I told myself, what did your mother do with it? I screwed up my eyes in concentration as I forced myself to go back in time until I saw her slipping the envelope surreptitiously into the hall cupboard drawer.

Would my father have thrown them out? No, I did not think so. My mother might have thought his parents were beneath her, but he had never shown any shame at them being simple people.

Back to those boxes again, I told myself. If he had kept them, they must be somewhere in there. I was right, for in amongst the heap of paper I had delegated to the rubbish pile were several thick envelopes. 'Got them,' I muttered. Flicking a finger under the edge of the envelopes, I found both letters from my grandmother as well as an assortment of black and white photographs.

'Thought you might like these,' she had written after telling my parents how lovely our visit had been and that she was already looking forward to the next one. Love to all us children had been included, as were scraps of information about the chickens, the old dog and how empty the house seemed without us all running around. A lump rose in my throat when I imagined her sitting at the kitchen table, her brow furrowed as she tried to think of interesting things she could share. She must have pictured my mother reading them out to us after supper and hoped that in return we would write back to her. I thought of how disappointed she must have been when she did not receive a reply from us, thanking her for sending them.

For not only had my mother not read the letters to us, she had not placed even one of those photos in her albums. No, she had not wanted to show her friends the small cottage where her in-laws lived. Certainly, she would not have wanted them to see the caravan with its outside kitchen tucked under a protective covering or the small outbuilding that housed the lavatory. This, combined with my grandparents' weather-beaten faces, would have given more than a hint of my father's origins. Without seeing those pictures, my mother must have been sure, no one would have guessed that Dad, with his smart clothes and polished accent, originated from gypsies – a race my parents' smart friends despised.

My mother's snobbery explained something I had almost missed. My well-turned-out English grandmother was in the wedding photos, but neither of my Scottish grandparents were anywhere to be seen.

My mother must have been determined to keep my father's roots well-hidden.

No doubt they had been told the wedding was just a small registry office affair, though I am sure my grandmother knew deep down what the real reason behind their lack of invitation had been.

I felt rage then at my mother's selfishness. Those pictures, unlike the ones she had kept, were not meant to be hidden away. They were meant to evoke happy memories, bring a smile to our faces as we passed them around before choosing one or two to frame and place where they would be seen by friends and family. They showed love, and not just for us but through some of the snaps of the river and the blue-tipped mountains they demonstrated a love of Scotland as well. They were so completely different from the posed ones my parents had taken.

Each one of theirs was carefully shot. There was never a sign of a tear or a frown on our childhood faces.

I thumbed through more of the photos showing Andy and me, some family picnics, and although shot through a cheap camera, there had been a certain skill in how my grandfather had managed to captured the rugged beauty of Scotland.

There was one of my parents, where my mother, her hair loose and her clothes casual, must have been unaware that her photo was being taken. My father's arm was around her shoulders and she was looking up at him and laughing at something he had said. I wonder now what it was. For all my memories of her have very little laughter in them. She looked happy and relaxed. I thought then that this was the woman she was meant to be.

There were a few more of my parents and, like the ones in the album, there was my dad with his sparkling eyes and good-humoured smile. There was not even one that showed he was anything but what people believed him to be, a kind, loving husband and father. But then maybe he had persuaded himself that was what he was. In the years I knew my mother, she, I have little doubt, believed it. Another picture of two small children, who with their mops of curly black hair and bright blue eyes looked so alike, they appeared to be twins: Andy and me. I felt tears prick my eyes as they do every time I think of how we were not just then, but for so many years. It was not so much that we looked alike; even in the photo our closeness could be seen: a closeness that never diminished.

More photos of us outside our grandparents' cottage until I came to one that for some reason sent prickles down my spine.

At first glance it was an innocuous enough image of two children happily engrossed in those simple things that small children do. Andy is sitting on a rug, clutching one of his toy cars in his hand, while I am standing by the garden fence. I'm holding on tightly to the top rail of the metal fence as I peer over it at something that has caught my eye. At that age between toddler and child, I was still not quite steady on my feet. Judging by the photo, I was determined to remain upright.

As I held the photo, memories flooded back and I felt my heart drop. An old fear had slid into my body, causing my mind to tumble like skittles at the ten-pin bowling centre. My breath started to come in short gasps and I felt my hands begin to tremble.

'Don't be silly,' I told myself, crossing the kitchen to switch on the kettle. 'It's only an old photograph, there's nothing there for you to start having a panic attack about. A cup of tea will sort you out, you've been looking at the past for too long.' Quickly, I poured boiling water over a teabag, added sugar and milk, then impulsively helped myself to a chocolate biscuit to provide comfort and walked over to the settee and sat down.

What was it about that picture that was so disturbing for me? Hard as I tried to remember, only an image, too faint to see, scratched the surface of my mind. It tormented me for the rest of the day, no matter how hard I tried to stop thinking about it. Even that night it stayed in my subconscious, making me toss and turn in my sleep. And through the night, like elusive butterflies dancing in the sun, vivid dreams flitted in and out of my mind.

I tried to force my slumbering brain to reach out, catch one and hold it tightly until I woke, but it refused to obey.

It was not until dawn was breaking that I realised the last images floating behind my lids were not part of a dream: they were memories.

They say every picture tells a story and when I sat up in bed that morning, I shivered. Finally, I knew the reason why the picture of me looking through the metal bars of the fence had been so disturbing. Oh yes, I also understood now where my fear of a light shining through my door and the sound of soft footsteps coming towards me had come from. A realisation that made me want to rush to the bathroom and vomit.

I wished I had never seen that photograph, wished that memory would just vanish into the air, and fervently wished I had never tried to find out every answer.

Too late now, I thought, as my mind transported me back over forty years until I was in the bedroom I had slept in as a child.

Decorated in pink and white with a silver mobile over the cot, it was a pretty room for a little girl. Not that my thoughts were lingering on the decor. Instead, I was seeing the toddler who had once been me, peacefully sleeping there. It was that night when her trust in those she believed were there to care for and protect her was shattered. Instead, she was shown a world that was no longer safe. As I sat upright, arms hugging my knees, I could hardly move as the scenes of what happened that night finally unfolded in my head.

I'm curled up in my cot. Something has woken me. It's the light from the landing shining through my door. I open my sleepy eyes, look through the bars and there is my father standing in the doorway. He places a finger to his lips as he makes the 'shhh' sound that tells me to be quiet, but I can't help letting a giggle escape my mouth.

I want to stand up, hoping he will lift me out. I roll over onto my back and, holding onto the bars, pull myself up so I can see him better.

Almost on tiptoes, he walks softly over to my cot and bends over it.

'Down you go, baby,' he tells me, placing firm hands on my shoulders.

My chubby legs fold until I am sitting on my behind, gazing up at him hopefully.

I feel his hand, warm and heavy, slide under my pyjama top. I'm not frightened, not then: he is my father, the man who holds my hand when we walk to the park, the one who sits me on his knee, his arm keeping me safe from falling, when he reads to Andy and me. The father I toddle towards when he returns home from one of his journeys. The one who lifts me high in the air and calls me his special girl and gives me presents to unwrap: a sparkling bag for my crayons, picture books and my favourite, a flaxen-haired doll from somewhere called Germany.

Him being in my room, his hand under my top, stroking my stomach, does not frighten me. Not then; I am still full of trust.

I like his familiar smell of tobacco and a lemony sharp scent.

I peek up at him through my lashes, trying to see where his other hand is. Is it, I wonder, behind his back, holding something for me?

And then something changes, something I don't like. His hand stroking my tummy is pressing me too hard. I try to wriggle away, my arms and legs jerking, but his hand is too heavy for me to move my body.

I see now where his other hand is: it's tucked in his lap and moving as though it has a life of its own. I can hear a funny noise, see his arm moving up and down, and hear sounds of him gasping as though in pain. When I look up at him, he's no longer the daddy I know. Not this man, whose flushed face is twisted into a strange grimace. He's not looking down at me; his gaze is focused somewhere over my head. I see his arm jerk, hear him give a louder gasp, then a soft groan as though in pain. I cry out in fear then.

'Shhh,' he says, patting my shoulder. 'Go to sleep, baby.'

And then he has gone and I am left whimpering into my pillow.

The picture starts to dim. I can hear my mother's voice calling out to him, but of course I have no recollection of the words she said. My imagination though can fill in the blanks. Remembering her attitude to me when I was a little older, I'm sure there was a note of impatience in her voice, not just because I was awake but that my father was giving me attention.

Attention that belonged to her. For once the children were in bed it was 'our time, your father's and mine,' she termed it for as long as I knew her. We were all aware of what she meant. She wanted her husband to herself and resented any interruptions, including those made by a child crying out from a bad dream.

I can hear her voice clearly in my mind: 'What's wrong with her now?' and him answering, 'Just a bit of teething, nothing to worry about.' Then, with confidence that my mother was satisfied with his answer, he would have poured them both a drink.

She never asked what had made me whimper that night but then she never did ask what was wrong when, over the years, my sobs echoed through the house. And I never confided in her as to what he had done that night – I was still too young to talk.

Did it happen more than once? I asked myself.

Did he often come into my room when I was asleep, stroke me and then grip himself with excitement?

Was it difficult for him to wait until I was just a little older, until he could begin to properly give in to his fantasies?

And the most important question of all that rose up in me: did he feel guilty?

The answer to all this is that I don't know. Any more than I know just when my mother began to see me as a rival for his affections.

No matter how much I reflect, I just don't know.

Chapter Three

There are times when having to get an active small child ready for school works in my favour, I thought, as I roused myself from my bed. No time to dwell on the past. As soon as Katy and I were both dressed and her hair brushed, breakfast was done and then, trying to act as normally as possible, I walked her to her nursery school. Luckily, she was so busy chatting about an art project, she did not notice my tiredness or my silence.

'Bye, Mummy,' she said chirpily as I handed her over to the young teacher. Bending down, I gave her a quick hug, happy that she had not yet reached the age of wriggling away from any public display of affection.

'See you later,' I replied, relieved that she seemed oblivious to my mood.

No sooner had Katy, along with several chattering preschool children, walked through the doors with hardly a backward glance in my direction than I walked back to my house as fast as I could.

I wanted to get those photographs out again.

'Leave them, Lynn,' said my rational voice.

But I knew I couldn't. I needed answers.

Once inside, before I had even placed the kettle on to make my morning coffee, I had them splayed out across the kitchen table. It was as though they were telling me that I needed to re-examine my past.

I thought of one of those inspirational quotes that popped up on my Facebook: 'The past is a good place to visit but not to live in'. Well, almost right, I thought, except mine was not even a good place to visit. Still, it had to be done.

Pulling another picture out of the envelope, I found myself back inside our family house again. There was the dining room where my parents entertained, with its gleaming mahogany table and sideboard. It was also used for what my mother termed 'family dinners', a ritual she insisted took place when my father returned from every one of his overseas trips.

He worked for an international haulage company. Not that as a child I had any understanding of what that meant. Only that his job took him away from home for up to a week at a time. This was something that made me happy and should it take him away for any longer than a week, I was even happier!

My mother, however, was far from content when he was absent. Instead of having more time for her children, if anything, she had less. Oh, meals were cooked, clothes washed and ironed, baths supervised and hair brushed, but she seldom read to us or suggested we all sat down and watched something on television together, things that as I grew older I wished for, as I did her affection. Whereas she was warm and loving towards Andy, few cuddles came my way. In fact, the only time I felt any closeness to her was when she trimmed my nails or untangled the knots in my thick hair. Then, just for that short time, I would lean against her, inhale her scent – a mix of soap and perfume – and just feel there was some intimacy between us.

An intimacy that always ended far too soon for the needy child I was.

'All done, now into your pyjamas with you,' she would announce in an overly bright voice the moment the last tangle was smoothed or the last nail cut, before not so gently pushing me aside and standing up. It was as though she found being close to me abhorrent.

Once Andy and I were in bed she would pop her head round our bedroom doors, turn off our lights and say goodnight before going back downstairs.

I never heard her go into Gavin's room. Even though he was ten years older than us he was expected to be in his room at the same time as we went to bed, although I think he was happier away from all of us.

I did not have to wait for my mother to tell us when my father was due back. Her behaviour spoke for her. The day before she expected him, she would be humming softly to herself as she went into a frenzy of domestic activity.

'Your father's coming home tomorrow,' she would tell us, her face lit up with a rare smile. This announcement did not cause any whoops of delight from us but she ignored the fact that not one of her three children shared her enthusiasm. In fact, there was complete silence for several minutes as it sank in that our freedom was coming to an end.

While my mother baked and cleaned with sudden vigour, we had to fend for ourselves. Gavin was given the task of making our lunch, which usually meant him opening a tin of baked beans.

On the morning of my father's impending arrival, my mother would disappear into the bathroom with an armful of lotions. It was a good thing for us that we had a separate downstairs loo, for once in that room she must have indulged in every beauty treatment she could.

Passing the bathroom, I would smell the fragrance of bubble bath mixed with steam that wafted out from under the door and wonder what it was a grown-up did in there that took so long.

Once her ablutions were complete and she had wrapped herself in a big fluffy towel, she would go straight to their bedroom. Another hour would pass as, after placing rollers in her hair, she sat under the dryer, painstakingly painting her toe- and fingernails. I knew all that because once I was old enough, it had been my job to bring her up cups of tea, which she sipped at daintily to avoid smudging her fingernails as she transformed herself. It must have been the only time she ever asked my opinion, on everything from the colour of her nail varnish to which dress suited her the most.

'What do you think, Lynn?' she would ask, twirling around in the chosen outfit.

'You look pretty,' was my standard reply, which in fact she did.

Thirty minutes before he arrived, she would appear downstairs, wearing the dress she had shown me. Her face would be carefully made up, and her high heels, kicked aside during his absence, were firmly on her feet.

His first evening back was, my mother always told us, 'family time'.

'We will have a nice meal together,' she would say. 'Gavin can help lay the table and Andy and Lynn, don't get your clothes messed up before he comes now, will you?'

Dutifully, the pair of us, dressed in our Sunday best, would chorus, 'No, Mum.'

'Oh, and once supper is over, I'll let you put yourselves to bed. Just this once, mind, so I'll have to trust you to brush your teeth properly.'

A statement that always gave me some relief even though I knew it was only temporary.

The moment we heard his car draw up, we clustered near the hall. And then he was there, case dumped at his feet, his arms wrapped around my mother. Then it was my turn for a hug and a lift in the air. 'My special girl' was his endearment, a 'Hello, little fellow' to Andy as his hair was ruffled and a quick pat on Gavin's shoulder and a nod towards his case: 'Gavin, could you ... ' And before the sentence was complete, Gavin had picked it up and carried it up the stairs.

Our family night had begun.

Throughout the meal, I tried to tune out my parents' conversation. My mother was smiling and asking him all about his trip as though every detail was of vital importance to her. He replied, telling us how well he had got on with the people he had met, implying with every comment that they thought he was pretty special. The sound of cutlery scraping on plates was, I thought, more interesting than that. Much as I wanted to, though, I could not ignore the occasional question thrown in Andy's and my direction.

'We all missed you,' my mother would say, before turning to us for confirmation, 'didn't we, children?' A question to which she received the only answer she wanted to hear – a chorus of 'yes' – before she gave her husband a smile to confirm that the house was not the same without him. Which of course was true, but not in the way she meant.

Once the meal was finished, the plates were cleared and my mother complimented on her cooking, it was time for the next ritual: the handing out of presents.

'Now,' my father would say to Gavin, 'go back upstairs and fetch my bag. There's something for each of you in it.' Dutifully, Gavin would leave the table to fetch the same case he had taken up earlier.

The first small parcel my father pulled out of the case was always for my mother.

'Oh, John, you shouldn't have!' she would cry each time she unwrapped the gift-wrapped boxes that usually contained perfume.

If he ever bought her something more intimate, we certainly never saw it.

The words 'For my special girl' announced that my present was next. With a flourish, another brightly coloured parcel was pulled from the bag and handed to me. When I was small, wondering what he had bought me would have made me feel a flash of excitement as I stretched out my arms to receive it, I expect. I have no memory of that though, for my mind will only take me back to the time after my trust in him had vanished.

Of course, even when I had reached the stage when I no longer wanted anything from him except to be left alone, I knew better than not to show my appreciation. So, regardless of what I uncovered once I had removed the wrapping, I would force my eyes to widen, give a gasp of what he perceived as pleasure and say, 'Oh, thank you, Dad! How did you know that was what I wanted?' before giving him the widest smile I could manage.

I was painfully aware that anything less would win his displeasure. My father's good mood, as we were only too aware, could disappear in a flash – and one of us would suffer for that.

Andy's parcel always contained something he had dropped the odd hint about, another miniature car to add to his collection or a toy plane. Gavin, whose present was always the one pulled out last, usually received a sensible article of clothing. Unlike our gifts wrapped in colourful paper, his was still in the shop's bag. He always flushed before stammering out his thanks as though it was something he had been wishing for. I'm sure what he really wanted to receive was a thoughtfully wrapped box that might give some indication that my father cared for him, but he never did. Though sensibly, if Gavin ever felt disappointment, he hid it well and, like us, expressed his thanks.

'Now, say thank you to your father for remembering each of you when he was so busy working,' my mother would say at the end of the meal. Again, we turned towards him and chorused in unison, 'Thank you, Dad,' trying to look happy that he was back there with us.

Once the presents had been distributed and all the thanks that was possible to give spoken, my father, as he did every time he returned home, walked over to the sideboard and poured drinks for my mother and himself. That was the signal to tell us family time was over.

Each time I heard the sound of their drinks being poured, I crossed my fingers tightly behind my back. 'Please don't let Mum change her mind about letting us put ourselves to bed,' I would silently mutter. Thankfully, she seldom did. She just glanced at us expectantly, which was her way of saying, 'Time for you all to go, I want my husband to myself now.' Needing no encouragement, the three of us said our goodnights and made ourselves scarce as fast as possible.

I always felt a little of my tension leave me as I climbed up the stairs. For every time my father caught my eye, I had felt dread circling my body. Dread that he would offer to put Andy and me to bed.

There were times when we were already upstairs before he arrived home but just knowing he was due would cause my stomach to tie itself in knots. Even hearing his car draw up and his voice booming up the stairs was enough to make goose bumps appear on my arms.

It would not take long for him to take charge of Andy and my bathtimes. Times that I have tried to forget, but even now, I remember them only too well.

Chapter Four

Those photos had taken me to a place where I no longer felt like the competent woman I see myself as. My trip to the past had woken all the residues of my childhood fear. As I sat at the kitchen table, I was powerless to stop the kaleidoscope of images of the childhood I had shared with my brothers from flooding my mind. I was back to being that small child again, afraid of the sounds of his footsteps in the dark and his voice too. But then those first two fears never really left me, did they?

I always knew when it would be him who would put us to bed. A couple of days would pass but that failed to lull me into a false sense of security. I was only too aware that he was just biding his time. Whenever I was in the same space as him, I could feel his eyes following me.

I can see my small self now, standing awkwardly in the sitting room, waiting to be told to leave and that it was time for bed. It was hearing the sound of a drink being poured. It was him catching my eyes as his arm went around my mother's shoulders that caused the prickles of fear to run up my back. I knew what his next move would be: a kiss bestowed on top of her head, followed by the words I dreaded hearing, ones I knew off by heart. They only take a few seconds to utter. Each time he did, his eyes met mine; knowing, mocking eyes that made me tremble as he said, 'Leave them to me, Kathy. You've done enough now, I'll sort out Lynn and Andy's baths. Put your feet up for a while. I'll call you when they're in bed, then you can come up to say goodnight.'

'Thank you, darling,' was nearly always her grateful answer. An answer that for a short time I believed was said in all innocence. A little later on though, I had good reason to question that. She must have seen my unwillingness to go with him, but chose to ignore it. Instead, she simply sat in her chair, watching her husband, with a wide, complacent smile, leading her two small children firmly out of the room.

I hated the sound of the bathwater running, the smell of the bubble bath as it slid from the bottle, taking off my clothes and standing there naked, while his eyes ran up and down my torso. But my biggest hate of all was getting into that water.

'You first,' he would always say to my brother as he picked him up.

Once Andy was in, it was my turn. I would flinch as his large hands slid under my bottom before, with a quick lift, I was plonked down, facing my brother. Before Andy began to understand why I disliked bathtime so much, he just grinned with pleasure at being able to splash both of us. Bathtime then was just a game to him, one that my father seemed to enjoy taking part in. With his sleeves rolled up on his muscular arms, soap in one hand and flannel in the other, he would wash Andy's back and laughingly flick water over us before handing my brother the flannel and telling him to get every bit left squeaky clean.

'You can finish the rest yourself, Andy,' he always said, the tone of his voice and the sideways look he gave me implying that

I, on the other hand, being a year younger, was not so proficient in washing myself.

'All finished then?' he would ask with a smile after, it seemed, less than a minute.

'Yes, Dad,' my brother would say before lifting up his arms to be helped out.

Once Andy was on the bathmat, he would rub him dry and then tell him to get into his pyjamas.

'Off you go to bed, son,' he would say each time, giving him a pat on the shoulder. 'Your sister, as usual, has not washed properly! She leaves out bits every time. Still, she's younger than you and she's a girl,' he would add with a conspiratorial wink. And Andy would beam up at our father, who was still his hero. 'Oh, and you can play with your toy cars until I've finished here. She'll only be a few minutes. Then I'll tell your mother to come up and tuck you both in, so don't fall asleep now, will you?'

Of course, my brother would not fall asleep, not when he had permission to play with his favourite toy racing cars. Nor would he notice that our father spent more than just a few minutes making sure that I was clean.

A sinking feeling would rise in my stomach every time I heard the sound of the door clicking shut behind him. It told me I was alone with Dad.

'Now, let's get you sorted out,' he would say as he crouched over my small body. 'Mmm, which bit needs cleaning the most, do you think, Lynn?' he would ask, running his hands over me. 'Ah, that bit!' and then, slick with soap, his fingers would disappear under the water.

How my body froze as I felt his hand sliding around my lower half until he slid it in between my legs and ran his fingers against those tiny delicate folds. Even then, small as I was, I felt shame at him touching me there. I did not know why it was wrong, but instinct told me that it was. By then I had also understood it was not something I was ever to talk about. My father had made this very clear to me.

'There are some things that are private,' he'd told me, 'things that nice little girls never talk about. Do you understand?'

I didn't, but still, I nodded my head.

'Good girl,' he would say. 'Because if you tell anyone, you would make your mother and me very sad. And you don't want to do that, do you?'

I just shook my head. Even then I recognised a threat thinly disguised as a question. I understood that 'sad' was just another word for 'angry'.

There were evenings when my heart was in my mouth as I stood waiting for him to lift me into that bath. Then, instead of keeping me there and sending my brother to his room first, he would haul us both out, one after the other, and quickly towel us dry. Of course, I felt relief when that happened, but even then the tension did not leave my body until my pyjamas were on and I was back in my room.

No, bathtimes were not fun times for me: I simply dreaded them.

It has taken me years to grasp the truth of just what game he was playing with me. Little by little, I was changing: becoming a nervous child, one who was always worried about doing something wrong. One he was determined to make totally compliant to any suggestion he made. A puppet child, who jumped every time he pulled her strings.

Like a cat with a mouse, he played his game of letting me out of the bath first one night, keeping me behind another, until not knowing what was going to happen next increased my anxiety. Once he felt the fear in me, his touching became more aggressive. Instead of his hands just stroking and touching, a hard finger would probe the tender place between my legs until he slid it just inside me. That hurt, making me bite my lip to stop a gasp of pain and shock escaping my mouth. For when I did, he would become annoyed.

'Oh, stop being a silly little girl, Lynn! Just got to get you clean, now stop with your nonsense,' he would say crossly while I sat shivering in the cooling water, my eyes fixed on the window behind him.

I know he felt me flinch: he knew he had hurt me and that I hated what was happening. But then I think it was his growing control over me that added to his enjoyment.

Once out of that bathroom, I would go to Andy's room. It was there when my mother, immaculate as ever, would sometimes appear to read us a bedtime story. If she was not in the mood to do so, she would just tell me to go to my own room, say goodnight and check our lights were turned off. If she noticed that I was subdued or even tearful, she never asked what was wrong, just pretended she hadn't noticed.

I think it was around then that my nightmares began, ones that woke me in the night. I can't remember now what they were about, just that they frightened me. I do wonder though where the contents of them came from. After all, I had not reached the age where I watched unsuitable films on TV or could read stories too old for me. Nor did I mix with children who told me about monsters. Perhaps it was my fear that conjured them up because somehow, large menacing shapes, all intent on harming me, visited my dreams. Then there was another one that, until I entered my teens, visited me regularly and over the years invaded my sleep. I was in a room with no furniture and no door; I was very small and I never grew any bigger. In that dream, the walls reached high above my head. As I searched for a way out, they would start moving, coming closer and closer, until, with outstretched arms, I tried to hold them back. Then, just before they crushed me, I woke with my stomach churning, white-knuckled hands clasping the bedclothes.

When I was little, I understood it was pointless crying out for my mother to come although that's what I really wanted. Someone who would stroke my hair, tell me it was only a dream and that nothing bad was going to happen before, with a hug and a kiss, she tucked the once-rumpled bedclothes around me. Even more importantly, she might have left a light on or stayed with me until I fell asleep. I had come to believe the darkness concealed what was hidden in the shadows and it frightened me. But none of that would happen for disturbing my parents would only incur their wrath, I knew. Instead, I curled into a ball and muffled my cries with the pillow.

Although I thought then that nothing could be worse than what my father was doing to me, I still believed he loved me, a belief I carried for far too many years. As an adult, I know what love of a child means. It means that more than anything, you want to be sure that they are both happy and safe.

I was neither.

Chapter Five

Our parents played the 'perfect family' charade extremely well. Not only were they generous hosts, they made sure that neither Andy nor I appeared to want for anything.

'My goodness me, not another new dress, Lynn!' a beady-eyed friend of my mother's, who I had been told to address as 'Aunty', would exclaim nearly every time she visited. I wanted to move away from her, for once the remark was made, her long, manicured nails would dart out to pluck at the fabric, no doubt trying to assess both the quality and the cost.

'Very nice, dear! You *are* a lucky little girl, aren't you?'

With some of her curiosity satisfied, she would move her inquisitive gaze to Andy. Now it was his turn to answer her questions.

'And what is that you are holding, dear?'

Andy, his dimples showing as he gave her a winning smile, would hold out his latest toy for further inspection.

'Ah, I can see that it's brand new. Not your birthday, is it?' she would ask, knowing all too well it wasn't.

'No,' my brother would reply with a giggle. 'Dad always brings us home something when he's been away.'

What we never told those prying family friends was that my new dress had been put on for their benefit and any toy that Andy was playing with would be consigned to the toy box just as soon as they departed. Those were secrets that we knew better than to mention so we just smiled politely and, once again, established ourselves as being two little privileged children who, although rather spoilt, still had good manners. Not that they thought the same of Gavin.

They saw him as a rather sullen, overweight and clumsy teenager who, when asked a question, just mumbled a few monosyllables, while avoiding eye contact. Having done their duty by trying to include him in the conversation, they lost interest and turned their attention once more to Andy and me.

Gavin must have heard them telling my parents, for Andy and I heard it often enough. With our dark curly hair and blue eyes, we were just adorable – the pretty children who looked so like their handsome father.

Oh, of course presents were given to Gavin on his birthday and at Christmas. My parents and their friends did the right thing there. But I seldom if ever saw any affection or even a genuine smile going in his direction.

As children, Andy and I saw him not as an unhappy boy, but as a bully and we were united in our dislike of him. There had been times when we made overtures – after all, he was, as we had been told by our Scottish grandparents, our big brother. Like most children, Andy and I wanted to be liked. We were not to know that Gavin's jealousy started long before we could talk. By then, it was too deep-rooted to be changed. It did not take more than a couple of rebuffs for Andy and me to shrug and decide not to try again.

Our father, we knew, had little time for him – in fact, very few people did, it seemed. He never brought school friends home or asked permission to go to one of their houses to play or for tea. When school finished, he always came straight home. So, if he had no friends, we reasoned, then our not getting on with him had to be his fault and not ours.

Back then, I made no excuses for Gavin, I just did not like him. Andy was my brother, not him. I was all too aware of his smirks when our mother told one of us off for some minor misdemeanour and heard him snigger when one of us fell over his outstretched foot, which we all knew had been put there deliberately. For behind our parents' backs, he showed his spite. If he caused us to fall and scrape our knees, we learnt quickly not to cry. Tears running down our cheeks would only have given him satisfaction. Instead, we bit our lips and tried to look as nonchalant as possible.

Now, as I reflect on our early years, I can understand his feelings. What had happened to him was sad. No longer the centre of his mother's world, he was in fact hardly in it – he just did not fit anymore into the picture she had created of the perfect family. Even if he wanted to kick a ball, he did so alone. When I think back to those times, I can see him so clearly: a large, lonely boy in a big garden.

One who, feeling he had been pushed too far, eventually tired of turning the other cheek.

Memories of my childhood are now flooding my mind. Some are so faint that they slide from my grasp, others make me shudder. All of them seem to belong to another person, one who lived a different life from me, though.

It is the photos that make them real. They have padded them out and made them clearer. Each time I handle them, I ask myself, am I doing the right thing? But I know I am. After all, it is our past that helps form us, but later, it is our determination that turns us into our own person. So, look, I tell myself, and be proud of what you have achieved. Search for some nice memories, you know there were some. Weren't there days when we did normal family things? A scenic drive in the car to nowhere in particular? I know there were visits to the seaside, Andy and I building sandcastles in the sunshine. At the end of the day coming home with pink flushed faces, traces of sand between our toes. And didn't our father sometimes take us all to the cinema? We saw *E.T.*, didn't we? And that was chosen for Andy and me, not our father's enjoyment. We were not always sent to our rooms either – what about those fish and chip suppers, where we all sat around the kitchen table?

It is just that over the years, the bad memories have coloured them and I feel incapable of peeling them away and only looking at the good ones.

There are small parts of my past that as a child made an impact on me. And those I have never forgotten. One of them is being absolutely stunned when I first came face-to-face with the proof of Gavin's secret talent. The others are the pictures of my mother I still carry in my head; the few times when I felt close to her. For me they are precious though even now she is an enigma to me. I still feel that I never really knew her and certainly I never knew Gavin. Handled differently, we could have been friends, but our parents made sure that never happened. There is not one photo of him in his teens but that does not stop me remembering how he appeared at the time Andy and I invaded his privacy.

When Gavin was not in the garden mooching around or kicking a ball desolately, he was upstairs. Andy and I were curious as to what he did in there. There was no TV or anything to play music on and I rarely saw him read. Surely, he did not just sit there?

'Well, he would have homework, wouldn't he?' I said when Andy brought the subject up.

'What, *him*? He's not sitting at that for hours, is he? I've never heard that he got high grades in anything. I mean, Dad was pretty angry, wasn't he, when he saw his last report. He called him stupid and a waste of time. No, he's up to something else in there. Let's go in and have a look,' Andy said, his eyes suddenly alight with mischief. 'He's not in, Mum's sent him to the shops.'

'He'll be cross,' I replied – and a cross Gavin was not someone I wanted to be near.

'Oh, come on, Lynn! Don't be a baby, you know you want to have a look. I'm going to anyhow.'

Needing no further persuasion, I followed my brother up the stairs to Gavin's room. Giving me another grin, Andy grabbed hold of the door handle and swung the door open.

I gasped at what I saw then; I would never have imagined it: this was why the door was always shut.

The walls were simply covered with hand-drawn pictures and paintings that must have taken him hours to create. Even as a child, I understood they were good. He had captured some of the dramatic scenery we had all seen in Scotland. There was one where he must have risen early to catch the morning mist rolling back over the hills. There were several of old buildings, every crumbling brick meticulously drawn. Every one of those pictures had a beauty of its own and not one reflected his inner rage. Thinking about them in later life, I realise once he had a brush or sketching pencil in his hand, he must have entered a different world to the one he lived in. There was one that drew me close enough to want to run my fingers over it: a delicate painting of my grandparents' old collie.

I hadn't even known he liked him. He must have though, for he had caught that expression of bliss on the dog's face that appeared whenever we scratched the backs of his ears.

I spotted a thick sketchpad leaning against the desk and just could not resist opening it up. Inside were more detailed drawings of trees, plants and a couple of small wild creatures: a rabbit hiding in the undergrowth, a bird taking flight, and the last one showed the moonlight catching the red of a fox's coat as it slipped away in the dusk. He must have been watching it through his bedroom window.

I found it hard to believe that this sullen, detached boy who we lived alongside could have created something so beautiful. Andy and I, unable to express the effect Gavin's painting had on us, just looked at each other guiltily before silently tiptoeing out. I think it was a kind of sadness we felt – all of that beauty hidden away in his room, with no one to admire it.

Our mother must have seen the pictures. Surely, like us, she had stood and felt moved by them? Why then did she never mention them? Later, I concluded it was the reason he had hung them on the walls: they were not just pinned up but arranged thoughtfully to show them to their best advantage. And he must have known it was a real gift he had. The art master would have told him that, surely? Then I had another thought, not a pleasant one: it would have been on his school report. How he must have wanted his mother to see that he was so much more than simply her oldest child, who always seemed to irritate her.

I just cannot comprehend why she did not wish to give him a hint of pride that her mentioning them would have. She must have been aware that Gavin craved her affection. He so wanted her to take notice of him – to talk, ask questions and make him feel that he was special to her. If she ever did, I never heard her. Did she resent the fact that at fourteen, he had lost his boyish looks? Although he never seemed to eat more than us his weight had ballooned, a problem that has continued throughout his life. In our mother's eyes he was the flawed child who spoilt the image of the perfect family.

I would hear her snap at him, 'Get out from under my feet!' when he tried to help clear the table. Or 'Do something useful, can't you?' when he wandered hopefully into her orbit. Terse comments that just made him look bewildered.

Being constantly criticised and mocked did not stop Gavin trying to win back the love he believed she once held for him. Andy and I were in the kitchen one day when he walked in from school. He was holding a thin cardboard folder in his hand, which he laid carefully on the table.

'Mum, I've brought you something,' he said nervously. 'It's a present I made you.' Opening it, he brought out a pen-and-ink drawing of a bird in flight. 'My art teacher was really pleased with it,' he added, 'told me I should take it home and give it to you to frame. Do you like it?'

Andy and I watched him looking at her hopefully.

'Why, Gavin, thank you,' she said with just the right note of surprise in her voice. 'It really is good,' and I saw him flush with pleasure. At last he had done something to please her.

'I tell you what, how about if you draw me another picture?'

His old smile broke out on hearing that, but how I cringed at what she said next as she glanced in our direction.

'I would really like one of your brother and sister, will you do that for me? That I would pin up,' she told him, placing the picture of the bird back in its folder.

I saw an array of emotions flit across his face: disappointment, followed by anger. His face reddened with temper. Even then I saw there was something else in his eyes, stronger than anger. I know now what it was: grief.

Grief for the loss of her love, and, perhaps, his for her.

Chapter Six

There was one use that our parents did have for Gavin: he was considered old enough to be our babysitter. That was the one time he was told that he was trusted; trusted enough to look after both the house and us. He could watch anything on TV he wanted to and help himself to food. They even managed to appear grateful that he would do it for them. Or maybe they were just a little grateful – after all, it was thanks to him that my mother could don a pretty dress and go with my father to visit friends or dine at the latest fashionable restaurant.

At first, he was proud of being trusted, I think. He valued their praise, but more than anything, there was the kiss our mother bestowed on his cheek before leaving. It was after her reaction to the drawing he had brought home for her that he finally saw through their temporary niceness to him: he knew that it only came in his direction when they wanted something. He must have felt so used and bitter for him to do what he did the last time he was left in charge.

That night, he showed just how deeply the years of hurt and resentment had damaged him. My parents left in a hurry. To our great relief, no bath that night – we were just to go upstairs, wash and put ourselves to bed.

No sooner had Andy and I heard the sound of the door closing than we rushed to the window and watched as they drove away.

'Let's go back downstairs and tell Gavin we want to watch television too,' Andy said with a grin.

'What if he says no?'

'He won't. I caught him smoking in the garden. He was bothered I would tell Mum. I told him he needn't worry, I had better things to do than become a sneaky telltale. Still, he won't want to upset us, will he, just in case I change my mind.'

'Oh, alright,' was my reply as the idea of watching the television was just too tempting to ignore. We waited a couple of minutes to make sure our parents were not returning for something they had forgotten, then made our way downstairs cautiously.

Andy was right: Gavin took no notice of us when we plonked ourselves down in the sitting room, he just looked indifferent to our presence.

'Hey, you two!' he said in a surprisingly friendly voice a couple of hours later when he noticed our heads were beginning to droop. 'Don't fall asleep. You'd better get yourselves off to bed, you'll get into trouble if you're caught down here when Mum and Dad get back.'

We were both a bit surprised by his tone being so friendly and even more so when he offered to make us a drink before we went to bed.

'You can drink it down here and then get up to bed,' he said. 'Just wait here and I'll go and make it.'

A little bemused, we waited on the settee while he took himself off to the kitchen. A few minutes later, he returned, carrying two mugs.

It was Andy who, having lifted the mug to his mouth, put it down quickly.

'It smells horrid,' he said.

Following his lead, I placed my hands behind my back.

'Don't want it,' we both said, 'it smells nasty.'

All of the friendliness left Gavin, leaving in its wake his dislike of us glittering in his eyes.

'Listen here, you ungrateful little tykes! I have let you watch television all night and made you hot drinks, now just drink them down then go to bed.' His voice had risen with anger and I shrank back on the settee, suddenly frightened by him.

'I made it especially for you!' he yelled when we did not do as we were told, and his clenched fist was raised angrily above our heads as he towered over us. Again, he shouted for us to swallow it, repeating he had gone to the trouble of making it especially for us. Indeed, he had. But his voice had risen so much that he did not hear the front door being opened or see our parents walking into the lounge.

'What's going on in here?' I heard my mother exclaim.

'He,' I managed to stutter, pointing to the two mugs still sitting on the floor beside us, 'wanted us to drink that. But it smells funny, Andy says.'

I saw Gavin's face drain of colour, the purple angry one suddenly white. His rage had been replaced by fear. It was our mother who picked one of the mugs up, held it to her nose and sniffed it.

'Gavin, what did you put in these?' she asked. Behind the coolness of her tone I sensed that whatever she had smelt in the mug was very bad.

'John, smell that,' she said and sat down as though she had not the strength to stand. I noticed she was trembling.

'You didn't swallow any of this?' she said, turning to us.

Knowing there was something terribly wrong, we just shook our heads.

'Kathy, please take them up to bed,' my father said. 'I'll deal with this.'

'Come,' she told us, unusually gently, 'let's get you both safely upstairs.'

I was expecting her to question why we were still up and to be annoyed with us. I had waited for it to be mentioned, but downstairs, neither parent had said anything about it. Nor did our mother say anything about us disobeying her when she put us to bed. From what I learnt later, they had more things to worry about than if we had watched TV all evening.

Instead of berating us, she sat us both down on my bed. Gavin had, she told us, been very, very naughty. He had played a prank, even if it was not a nice one. That was all. And it would be best for everyone if we forgot about it.

'No need to tell anyone about this, is there? Not friends, teachers or Grandma.'

'No, Mum, we won't,' we chorused, relieved that it was not us in trouble.

It was much later when I learnt that the word 'prank' was rather an understatement. Slowly, we discovered just what had been in that drink. When he had left us sitting sleepily in front of the television, Gavin had gone through the cupboards, looking for anything that would make us ill. What he had found, had we drunk it, would have done more than make us sick: he had mixed caustic soda with bleach, then tried to disguise it with hot chocolate and milk.

Thank goodness my brother had a sensitive nose! Just a mouthful of that would have had us sent to hospital and probably sent Gavin straight to a Juvenile court.

What I did know though was how severe the beating Gavin received that night was: his screams and pleas could be heard all over the house. Luckily for my parents, our house was detached so sounds could not carry through the walls. But it was not his cries that disturbed me so much as our mother's voice shouting for my father to stop, that he would kill him if he didn't. She sounded scared and I had never heard her like that before.

After that, there was an eerie silence and I fell into a deep sleep.

In the morning there was no sign of Gavin at breakfast. He was not at school for a week. A cold was the excuse given to us and the school, but I would think he was too bruised to be seen in public.

Andy and I were made to understand that we must never take anything from him, however tempting it looked – not a sweet, a cake or anything else. Again, our mother made us promise never to talk about what had happened and assured us that Gavin was very sorry. If she hadn't brought it up again we might have believed the word 'prank', but seeing her worried face, we understood it was more than that.

I did learn, through those parts of parental conversations that children are good at listening to, that a boarding school had been discussed as an option for him. I also heard my father say that he could not deal with Gavin; he had tried his best but he was an ungrateful boy, who resented him and his half-brother and sister. He insisted that he could see no other option.

I never knew what my mother said to make my father, if not change his mind, agree to her wishes for Gavin to stay. I can only think that in the end she knew some of the blame was hers and that she could not bring herself to send him away.

At least that's what I hope happened.

Chapter Seven

In the pile of photos that I had taken from the albums, I came across one of me when I was aged around five. Who took it and who had put it there, I wondered. I doubted it had been my mother. Then I remembered it was taken when my English grandmother came to stay. My mother said she wanted a break from the loneliness of living alone in that big house. Although she lived nearby, my grandfather had been dead quite a few years and every year, she still found the anniversary of his death difficult. She was a woman, who, with her smart clothes, carefully set hair and subtly applied make-up, was very different from my Scottish grandmother.

Looking at the small dark-haired girl who used to be me, I can tell by what I was wearing, a white cardigan over a pink and white gingham dress, that it was spring. Just holding the photo in my hand brings that day back into my mind vividly. Wanting to go outside, I had been peering through my mother's pale floating curtains. In the next-door garden was a chestnut tree, its cones of pink and white flowers in full bloom, but what caught my eye was the swing that hung from it. Something that Andy and I wished we had, but knew it was useless asking our father as it would spoil the perfection of our garden.

Gavin and Andy were at school, which I was not due to start until after the summer, and I was bored. Hearing my mother's voice, I wandered into the kitchen, where she and my grandmother were preparing food. I don't know now which meal it was for, but I do know it was my grandmother who brought up the subject of Sunday School and this is where I heard the word 'miracle' for the first time.

She had arrived a couple of days earlier and, although still saddened by the anniversary of the loss of her husband, had brought presents for us three children with her. Mine was the dress in the photograph. The night before, she had come upstairs to say goodnight and read a story to Andy and me. When it was finished, we were tucked up and given a soft kiss on the head, before being told to sleep tight. I had already decided I liked her very much.

It was when she and my mother sat down for a cup of tea and I was given a glass of milk that she again brought up the subject of Sunday School, at the same time glancing over the top of her spectacles in my direction. Was that different to the one I was going to start fairly soon, I wondered. Because all I knew about school was that I had been told that after the summer holidays, I would be starting in the Infants at the same school as Andy and he did not go to school on Sunday.

'Have the children started going yet?' she asked.

'Not yet,' came my mother's crisp reply.

'Not yet,' my grandmother repeated with some degree of impatience. 'Well, Kathy, it's time they did. It will be good for them, especially Lynn. It will prepare her for when she starts school.'

My mother didn't argue with her or say she was too busy on Sunday mornings to take us. But then I had noticed that she always seemed a little nervous around her mother. This time it was she who seemed to be seeking approval, not one of us.

'Yes, I was thinking of it,' she said a little defensively and I could tell by the glint in my grandmother's eye that she did not believe that remark.

'Oh, you'll be busy, I'm sure. I'll take her for you while I'm here, I want to go to the service anyhow,' was her firm reply.

I noticed my mother's shoulders stiffen, but instead of showing annoyance, she forced a smile on her face and said, 'Thank you.' It was not an offer that made her happy, I sensed. Once my grandmother returned to her own home she would expect my mother to keep up what she had started. Something I am sure now that my grandmother was only too aware of.

Sunday School, as far as my mother was concerned, must have meant Andy and me looking our very best, for the perfect family image still had to be kept up. It was she who dressed me in a blue pinafore dress, inspected my nails and brushed my hair, which was then tied in two bunches.

'You'll do,' she said.

As soon as breakfast was finished, my grandmother told us it was time to leave. Once outside the house, she took my hand.

'You'll like Sunday School,' she told me, 'lots of other children there. The minister's wife will read you a story. Then there will be some singing and when it's finished, I'll be waiting to take you home.'

She made no further comment, having deduced that neither of my parents were church-goers, something I am sure she disapproved of.

*

Once we arrived at the large grey stone building with its richly coloured stained-glass windows and huge double wood doors, she handed me over to the minister's wife, who was standing at the bottom of the stone steps. By her side was the minister, a kindly-looking man, who told me it was his wife who ran the Sunday School. My grandmother repeated what she had told Andy and me, that she would be there to collect us as both the service and Sunday School finished at the same time. Then, with a quick hug, she went into the church for the morning service.

While she had been talking to the minister's wife, other small children had arrived with their parents. When the minister's wife was ready, she briskly led her little flock not into the church where the minister was to give a service, but to a side room where small, scaled-down chairs had been placed in a circle.

My grandmother was right: I did enjoy myself, especially listening to the Bible stories. And there was one that made me sit up and take notice: the one where Jesus fed the multitudes. That is when I heard that word 'miracle'.

Eager to ask a question, I raised my hand.

'Yes, Lynn?'

'How do you find it?' I asked, finding the word too difficult to pronounce.

'Why, Lynn, we pray. God hears all our prayers and sometimes, if we pray hard enough, a miracle happens.'

'Miracle' was a word I tucked into my mind: I was going to ask God to send me one.

That night, after I had been put to bed, I climbed out of bed, knelt on the floor, put my hands together and prayed to the God who, although he lived above the clouds, could hear everything.

'Please let my father be the nice one every day,' I begged. 'Please stop him hurting me. And make my mummy happy all the time, then she'll be kind to us.'

I repeated that silent prayer every night while my grandmother was there. Even though I knew he would not come near me until after she left, I was determined to build up some credit with God. Once I had finished my prayer, I climbed back into bed, content that I had found out how to make the touching stop.

When my grandmother's visit ended, I felt tears prickle the back of my throat. The house had been a happier place with her in it. My father had been the nice father the whole week. Now all I could do was hope my prayers had worked.

But for one horrible moment that evening, I thought they hadn't.

'Bathtime,' he said and I recognised the expression on his face. He was almost impatient to get me up those stairs.

For once my mother looked up. Perhaps she had seen the fright on my face or caught the eagerness in his expression. Whatever it was, she said, 'I'll get them ready for bed, darling. You've had to put up with my mother for a week. I think you deserve a break from domestic duties.'

A look I could not fathom passed between them before he said, 'Alright, if you want to.'

My prayer had been answered. I felt like clapping my little hands together and saying thank you to God.

'Can I go to Sunday School this week?' I asked when I was climbing into bed.

My mother looked none too pleased at this request, but as her mother rang regularly and sometimes asked to speak to us, she had little choice but to agree (though in the end, she only took me a couple more times).

'Yes, of course I'll take you and Andy. Now, go to sleep,' she said.

I hoped that she would do as my grandmother did, give me a kiss goodnight, but she just switched off my light on the way out.

Were miracles permanent, I wanted to know. Or did they only happen once?

I just prayed for it to be forever. Surely if I went to Sunday School and said my prayers, God would see that I was good?

It seemed my prayer was answered again for the following morning my father was not there; he had left early to travel to Germany. And this time he would be gone for two weeks.

Although I wondered a little why he or my mother had not told me, the relief I felt by far outweighed that spark of curiosity. For fourteen nights I prayed and for fourteen nights, I totally believed my prayers had been answered. And then he returned and my childish innocence, of believing prayer would change my life, like smoke in the wind disappeared.

Remembering that part of my childhood made another memory jump into my head. A deeply buried memory that I had resisted looking at for so long, for letting it in would stop any feeling of forgiveness I have tried to nurture.

Those memories that the protective part of my conscious brain had for so many years tried to suppress were now churning in my head. My father, I was beginning to accept, was worse, far worse, than I had allowed myself to believe. One by one, the excuses I had made for him started to trickle away.

It was a couple of days after his return from Germany. He had acted the nice father to perfection. Hugs and presents. Telling us all how much he had missed us. And I, believing my prayers had worked, smiled back at him happily.

I could see him when I found the photos; I can also see him clearly now, coming into my room. Not the man I was afraid of, but the nice one that the small child I was then still believed existed. He was holding something in his hand and now I can recognise not just what it was, a large glass of squash, but the real reason he had brought it to me.

'Drink this, Lynn, it's good for you,' he said, his warm hands firmly covering mine as the glass was held up to my mouth.

It tasted nice, only there was too much of it.

'Drink it all up,' he told me when he saw that the glass was still half-full. 'It will do you good, it's full of vitamins.' Wanting to please him, I forced myself to swallow the rest of it down. 'Good girl,' he said, before picking up the glass and taking it downstairs.

I can't remember how old I was then. But not old enough to know what would happen if I swallowed that amount of juice before I went to sleep.

The first night I drank it, I woke up lying in a puddle. I was terrified – I had never wet the bed before and I knew my mother was going to be angry.

Jumping out of bed, my only thought was to try to clean it up before she saw what I had done. I thought of waking Andy and asking him to help me change my bed, but I knew neither of us was big enough to do that. Anyway, there was nowhere to hide the wet sheets and my mother would see if I just put them in the washing basket. And if I washed them and put them back on, I asked myself, but I realised then my mattress would be even wetter and she would be even angrier. Instead, I crept into the bathroom, tore off wads of toilet paper and tried to mop it up as best I could.

When I climbed back into bed I could feel the dampness from the sheets and my pyjamas. They were not going to be clean and dry by the time my mother came to tell us it was time to get up. There could be no hiding, for it was she who always came into our room to tell us to get dressed and come down for breakfast. That was the rule in our family: even if we were awake, we were to stay in our rooms until she told us to get ready.

That first time she surprised me. Instead of shouting at me, she just sighed and said, tight-lipped, 'Lynn, just get out of those stinking pyjamas,' before, with more sighs of disapproval and disappointment, she stripped the bed.

A few days later, my father came into my room with another glass of orange juice and a piece of chocolate. Again, his hands were wrapped over mine as he made sure every last drop was swallowed.

'Good girl,' he said with a smile and popped the chocolate in my mouth. 'Better not tell your mother,' he added with a wink. 'Not when she's trained you to brush your teeth regularly. It's our secret, alright?' And I smiled back happily. That was a nice secret.

That night, I dreamt I was somewhere warm and cosy. I remember as my eyes opened, I stretched contentedly – a contentment that vanished the moment I felt the wetness beneath me.

This time my mother really showed her anger.

'What is this all about, Lynn? Are you doing this to upset me?' she spat out furiously. 'Don't you think I have enough to do? Wetting yourself is for babies, not little girls. Now get out of my sight!'

The next time it happened, I was beside myself with fear. Tears simply poured from my eyes when my mother came into the room.

'Sorry, Mummy,' I pleaded between choking sobs.

She took no notice of how swollen my eyes were, just tugged the bedclothes off and told me to get dressed.

'You are not fooling me, Lynn. Once might have been an accident, but not three times. You're doing this on purpose, aren't you? You're a jealous little girl and just want more attention, don't you? Do you think I spend more time with Andy than you? Well, if I do, it's because he's a good little boy. You never do this when your father is away. Well, just wait till I tell him about this. If it's attention you want, he'll give it to you alright! Let's see what he thinks of your dirty habits.'

I wanted to beg her not to, to tell her it was an accident, that I had not meant to do it and that I would try harder for it not to happen again, but knowing my pleas would only fall on deaf ears made the words stick in my throat.

Once my mother went downstairs, I could hear her almost screaming with rage, telling my father about my nocturnal misdeeds.

'You have to do something about her, she's out of control,' were her final words.

Andy came into my room and placed his arms around me.

'Don't cry, Lynn,' he said, 'you know that only makes her madder.'

I laid my head on his shoulder as he hugged me.

'She's always so cross,' I said sadly, meaning that she was always cross with me.

Breakfast was tense; my throat felt so tight I could hardly swallow the cereal that my mother, without saying a word to me, had poured into my bowl.

'John, what have I just said? It's up to you to sort this out. Isn't that what we agreed?' She gave my father an unusually venomous look. 'She's becoming impossible and this latest trick, well, it's just all too much.'

'OK, leave it now, Kathy, I'll deal with it tonight. Rest assured, I'll make sure it doesn't happen again.'

His words sounded reasonable but I was not to be fooled. I knew something unpleasant was going to happen, I just did not know how bad it was going to be.

'Now, let's just have breakfast in peace,' said my father sternly, 'And Lynn, once you have finished yours, go to your room and stay there until I get home from work. Your mother is too upset with you to want you down here. You understand me?'

I just about managed to whisper a 'yes' before he told me to make sure I ate all my breakfast.

'It will have to last you till supper time,' he said with a cold smile. 'Your mother does not want to see you till then, so don't even think about slipping out of your room.'

As I glanced outside the sun was shining and the thought of being in my room all day brought a lump to my throat. I had not done it on purpose, I wanted to say, but I knew my parents' minds were made up.

I really can't remember how old I was at the time – had I started school then, or was it a weekend or part of a school holiday? It's difficult to go back through the years and put everything in order. But I do remember how frightened I was; too frightened to feel any hunger when lunchtime came and went. Being made to stay in my room all day was not to be my only punishment. I was just too young to see that my father's making me wait for him to return was the beginning of him refining the mental torture he inflicted on me over all my childhood years.

The adult person I am now has come to understand what he did: he gave me those drinks knowing what the result would be. Wetting the bed in my sleep made me bewildered. I knew it was wrong and could not understand why I was doing it. It took away my confidence but only seemed to increase his. Now he had an excuse to discipline me as much as he wanted. And he wanted that very much. Not that he had needed much of a reason to convince my mother of the necessity for that, I thought sadly. For the child I had once been really loved her so much.

That night, he came into my room, a tall frame towering above me.

'So, Lynn, why do you keep wetting your bed?' he asked in a calm voice that scared me more than if he had seemed angrier. 'Why don't you get up when you want to wee and go to the bathroom?'

I wanted to tell him I had dreamt about something that frightened me and then I had a peaceful feeling that I was lying somewhere warm; that when I woke, it was too late to go to the bathroom, I had already wet myself. But I could not explain all of that so I said what small children say when they can't find the words to express themselves, 'I don't know.'

'Well then, Lynn, you need to learn what happens to little girls who do something dirty. Take your knickers off!'

Startled, I looked up at him, not understanding what he meant.

'Lynn, I said knickers off, now!'

Still not realising what was going to happen, I pulled my white knickers down and stepped out of them while he moved from the doorway and sat on my bed.

'Now, come here.'

Nervously, I crept over to him. His arm shot out and I was pulled face down over his knees. I heard the crack and felt the pain of his hand descending on my bare bottom.

I had not been really hurt before. Oh, a quick slap across the backs of my legs, but that was all. This was different, this hurt a lot. I wriggled, kicked out and screamed until he picked up my knickers and shoved them in my mouth. My eyes must have been bulging with terror for I couldn't breathe, I was choking.

He removed the gag after a few moments and waited for me to stop gasping for breath.

'That goes back in if you scream like that again,' he told me. 'And the next time I won't take it out so quickly. Now, calm down and take what you deserve!' His hand grabbed the back of my neck and down I went again. Another stinging blow landed on my bottom, followed by another.

'That's enough for tonight,' he said, and without another word walked out of the room.

So that was the beginning of my thrashings. My father, over the many years he inflicted them on me, made sure that he did not leave bruises in places where they could be seen.

It was Andy who brought me up my supper and who sat on the bed and comforted me. My brother said what Dad had done to me was wrong but then he did not know what else my father did to me.

I did my best to avoid my father after that. His smiles and calling me his 'special girl' no longer brought happiness to my face.

'What's wrong?' he asked. 'Not still sulking about your punishment, are you?' To which I gave no answer. I was not old enough nor courageous enough, not then at least, to say how much I hated being anywhere near him.

He looked for every reason to punish me and I looked for every excuse to cease going to Sunday School.

God had failed me.

Chapter Eight

I think I was around nine when I learnt that my Scottish grandmother had died. I can still visualise the stricken expression on my father's face when he walked into the sitting room after taking the call.

For a moment or two both Andy and I were unnerved. We knew he was upset and his being upset was all too often followed by an outburst of temper, which one of us would bear the brunt of. But this time it was different: he looked completely shaken, the colour had drained from his face and his eyes looked as though they were moments away from tears.

When my mother, who had started to ask who it was on the phone, saw the expression on his face, she sprang to her feet and placed a hand on his shoulder.

'What's wrong, John?' she asked.

'Mum ... It's my mum,' he answered. 'She ... she's dead,' and as the words left his mouth, his whole body sagged and for the first time in my life I saw large tears falling from his eyes.

'You two,' she said to Andy and me, 'go to your rooms.' Very unusually, she added the word 'please' and tried to shield her husband from our astounded gaze. 'I'll come up a little later.' Bewildered and upset by what we had just heard and being sent out of the room without more of an explanation, we got up quickly from the table and went upstairs.

Gavin was already in his room and I wondered if I should knock on his door and say something – I knew how much he had liked our Scottish grandparents.

'Let Mum tell him,' Andy said when I asked him if I should.

It must have been very nearly an hour later before we heard our mother's soft footsteps approaching my room, where we lay huddled on the bed. By that time, we were both weepy; Andy had his arm around my shoulder and I was leaning against him. This was the first time we had heard the word 'dead' applied to anyone we actually knew.

'Is it true? Is Grandma really dead?' I asked the moment she came into our room.

'Yes,' she replied. 'She died this morning, it was sudden.'

I could not stop myself from sobbing any longer.

She came out with a few platitudes. Our grandmother had not suffered, she had gone in her sleep and yes, she had not been well for some time.

'Why did we not go to see her then?' Andy asked.

'Oh, Andy, no one knows when someone is going to die,' she answered. 'If your father had realised her illness was serious, of course we would have been there. It was not something we expected. Now,' she added, her face beginning to look a little sterner, 'I know you are upset, that you were both very fond of your grandmother, but you have to understand she was your father's mother so we must be strong for him. So, no more tears, alright?'

'OK, Mum,' said Andy.

'Yes,' I snuffled.

'Your father has decided to leave early tomorrow. He's going to drive to Scotland, he needs to spend some time with his father as well as arranging the funeral.'

'Why aren't we all going? Won't Grandpa want us all there?' Andy wanted to know and as he spoke, the forbidden tears sprang from his eyes again.

'I just told you, your father needs to spend time with his father. He'll be gone for at least a week. And Gavin and you both have school to go to, so your father and I have decided that it is better for him to go alone.'

'But what's going to happen to Grandpa afterwards?' I asked, thinking how lonely he must be in that cottage. 'I mean, who's going to look after him when Dad comes back?'

My mother's face went blank at that question and no answer was forthcoming. I could tell though that behind that expressionless mask something was bothering her that had little to do with the death of my grandmother, a woman she had made it very clear she had little time for.

All that week, Andy and I felt miserable. Not only would we never see our grandmother again, but without her being there, would we all drive up to Scotland for another holiday? We didn't really understand death. My English grandmother once told us that when someone dies, their soul goes to God's kingdom in heaven. But since my prayers had stopped working, my reasoning was that either God was deaf or there wasn't a heaven so I took no comfort believing that was where she was. Anyhow, her body would be in the coffin, I knew that much, so what exactly was a soul?

Gavin seemed even quieter than usual and was even more room-bound. I wanted to ask him how he felt; I could see that although he was trying to hide it, he was really upset as well. But then I had not got the confidence to talk to him about it. So, there we all were in that shiny clean house: three of us depressed and my mother permanently disgruntled, it seemed. There were quite a few phone calls that always seemed to put her in an even worse mood. I heard her saying tersely, 'What! How long for, John?' and whatever the reply was, she clearly did not like it. Not long before my father returned there were several more calls. One that I managed to overhear was her almost hissing with anger into the phone as she spat out, 'For heaven's sake, John! Don't you think I have enough to do?'

Whatever his reply, it caused her to slam down the phone while her cheeks flushed crimson. Catching sight of me and realising I had heard her did not improve her temper either.

'You, Lynn, find yourself something useful to do! And stop sneaking around, listening to calls that have nothing to do with you. Now, scram!'

And scram I did.

That frustrated anger of hers might have come in our direction often, but I had never heard her speak to my father like that before. I wondered exactly what he was asking for that had made her just about vibrate with rage. What could have been annoying her so much?

I was soon to find out.

She waited until we were all eating supper in the kitchen before she told us. 'Your grandfather's coming to stay with us for a while,' she announced flatly, 'so you can help me clear out that room your father uses as an office. He can sleep in there.'

I think all three of us were pleased, because we all liked our grandfather, but we knew better than to show it. We could tell with just one glance at her stony face that she did not share our feelings. I wanted to ask how long he was going to stay with us but knew that would not be a good idea either. Instead, it was Gavin who asked, 'When do you want the room cleared out, Mum?'

'Over the weekend, and your brother and sister can help. Just put all the stuff in there at the back of the garage, then make sure it's vacuumed and dusted everywhere,' she told us wearily, 'your father will be having a good look at it when he arrives.'

'Why is Grandpa not sleeping upstairs?' questioned Andy.

'More private for him down here. Anyhow, old men need the bathroom through the night and I don't want to be woken by that, I suppose, any more than he would want to disturb us. And the room is right next to the downstairs toilet so it's easier for him as well.'

Easier for him to be put into that little dark room when we had a big guest room upstairs? Easier for her, more like it, I thought, feeling angry with my mother and her unkindness. Going to the bathroom in the middle of the night was hardly going to wake the household, was it? Those thoughts I was sensible enough to keep to myself.

'Where's his dog going to sleep?' Andy asked.

'The dog has been rehomed,' my mother told us brusquely.

'Why?' I asked, because when I pictured my grandfather it was always with the dog by his side: they were inseparable. 'Didn't Grandpa want to bring him?'

'He's not a dog that would be happy on a lead,' my mother explained. 'He's used to fields, not busy streets and parks.' An explanation I did not believe. There were plenty of big dogs being exercised in the nearby park. Anyhow, the dog was trained to walk at heel and at night, he was content just to lie by my grandfather's feet. Still, there was no point in arguing with my mother or saying that as Grandpa had just lost his wife, wouldn't it have been kinder to have invited his other companion to stay too? But then few nine-year-olds have a voice to sway parental opinions so I turned away and said nothing more.

All of us worked together that weekend. Gavin seemed happy enough to be helping; there was even the odd friendly word thrown in our direction. There is nothing like a common purpose to ease the conflict between siblings. And he knew, I've since learnt, that our lives were also not so easy as he had once believed.

It must have been just over a week later when my father's car pulled up. We were all out of the door to greet them as soon as we heard it turning into the driveway, though I think in my mother's case it was more to oversee where the luggage my grandfather had brought with him was going to be put. Both men opened their doors and, my father sprang out, but I noticed how stiffly Grandfather manoeuvred himself out of the vehicle.

It seemed in that short time since we had been in Scotland he had turned into a frail old man. The last time I had seen him, he had been upright, with his cap firmly on his head and his trousers held up by braces, and was whistling to call his dog. He knew we wanted to say goodbye to the collie, as well as our grandparents, when we were leaving.

My grandmother was by his side then, her arms full of bags containing homemade cake, scones and sandwiches packed up for our journey. A lump formed in my throat as I pictured her in her flour-dusted apron saying, 'I'll be seeing you all next year,' and how she had smelt of baking and lavender when she hugged me goodbye.

He too had enveloped us in his arms and pressed a few coins in each of our hands. As we drove off, I looked through the back window of the car. He was standing there, a broad smile on his face, waving us goodbye.

This time when he hugged me, I could feel his ribs through his Aran sweater. He even smelt different, not of the fresh air and pipe smoke that I associated with him, but of something else – I think it was the scent of sadness.

My father's car was crammed with boxes, carrier bags and one battered old suitcase.

'The children can unload that,' my mother said, plastering a friendly smile on her face. 'Gavin, you take the suitcase and you two,' she said, turning to Andy and me, 'can pile everything else into the back of the garage. It can go alongside the stuff you took out of the room. You can sort through it later when you are feeling up to it,' she told Grandfather, 'but for the time being, it can stay in there.'

'Thank you, Kathy,' he said politely. 'I hope I've not caused you too much trouble.'

'Not at all,' was her simpering answer, but out of the corner of my eye I could see her thin-lipped look of disapproval.

'Yes, take the suitcases upstairs,' my father nodded to Gavin.

'Oh,' my mother said lightly, 'I've turned that office of yours into a bedroom. You hardly ever use it and I thought it would be more comfortable for him than going up and down the stairs.'

'Well, I suppose that will do for the time being,' my father said and then uttered the words that made my mother blanch, 'but I'm going to have a studio flat built above the garage for him.'

She made no comment but I could see the telltale signs of her anger. Her back stiffened as she walked into the house, without saying another word.

I learnt a little later that the cottage that he and my grandmother, Violet had taken so much pride in was in estate agents' hands. All the furniture had been taken away, as had our grandmother's clothes. My father had sorted that out. And I thought how seeing those possessions, so lovingly collected over the years, being taken away must have been one of the saddest parts of my grandfather's loss.

It's only when I look at photos that dim memories of my grandmother on my father's side come to life. Hair scraped back in a bun, a trim figure wrapped in an apron that only seemed to come off on Sundays and a smile full of love.

My memories of my grandfather are clearer, because my father did build the room above the garage, where he stayed with us for several years. And over time I think even my mother began to appreciate his presence.

*

There was nothing my grandfather enjoyed more than reminiscing about the past. Colourful stories simply poured out when he was alone with his spellbound audience of two, Andy and me.

I heard that both he and his wife were children of Spanish gypsies.

'We lived in the caravan you all stayed in before we managed to buy the cottage,' he told us. 'It was where we started our married life and we could not bear to get rid of it. Still, it came in useful when you all came to visit, didn't it?'

Another time he told us how our grandmother had been selling heather and reading fortunes when they met. That was what gypsy women did, he said, and the men did odd jobs: worked on farms, fixed bits of machinery, whatever work they could find. Then at night, they would all sit around a fire while the women cooked meals.

'We never had indoor kitchens, it was all done outside. The lavatories and showers were rigged up each time we found a place to stay for a few weeks. Yes, my dears, it was a traveller's life alright. But your gran and I wanted something more, to put down roots and when we had children, to make sure they had a decent education. And get respect. You know, gypsies were seen then as being rogues and thieves, not people who just liked to be free, and that was not a future I wanted for our children.'

He told us that it was a life he wanted to escape from and when he met my grandmother, he knew he had to find a proper job and stay in one place.

Andy and I thought the life he described sounded an exciting one and were always urging him to tell us more.

'Don't tell your mother about those stories,' he would say. 'I know she doesn't like to hear about it. But have a look in the mirror. Where do you think all that dark curly hair came from, eh? That's your Spanish roots showing alright!

'Did you know that your dad has three brothers – well, half-brothers, like you have Gavin?'

No, we didn't, we indicated with shaking heads.

'Thought not. I doubt your mother wants them around here. Your gran had been married before I met her. She must only have been about fifteen when she was given to her husband.

'She was a widow when we met. Five children in just over five years she had, but the two little girls died when they were just wee ones. Bonny she was though, even having had those children and the loss of the bairns and her husband when so young. And of course I fell in love with her. Oh, I knew it was a lot to take on, but I wanted it all done properly, so I married her. And you know, Andy and Lynn, I loved those children like my own. And then your dad came along. He was your gran's last child.

'Now my father, he was a very different man than me. He found out my mother was pregnant and what did the swine do?'

I just shook my head for then I had not heard of unmarried people making babies.

'Why, he ran off to Spain and was never heard of again. Well, gypsy folk don't take kindly to that. They like their women married. Her parents found another man for her. He married her and it was he who brought me up.'

'Was he good to you?' I asked.

Maybe then I should have asked what he meant by the curt response of 'no' that we received. But then children did not ask such personal questions. He clearly did not want to talk about his stepfather. Instead, he changed the subject.

'Your father is the only one we had together. That doesn't mean we didn't still love the others, but he was special. We could tell he was going to amount to something almost straight off. He was so bright, another reason we wanted to settle so he could get good schooling. He was not going to lead a traveller's life, Violet and I were adamant. He did well at school too. A hard worker, your dad is. And now he's a good provider, isn't he? I mean, you two and your ma hardly want for anything, do you?'

'I don't think he likes Gavin much,' I ventured.

'No? Well, perhaps he's not an easy boy now, is he? Even so, your dad keeps a roof over his head, gives him pocket money, buys him decent clothes,' and here, Grandfather looked at Andy and me sternly. 'He's a good man, your dad, and I'll never hear different.'

And for the rest of the time he lived with us, he never did. Nor after that comment of mine did he tell me anything else about the man who had married his mother.

Chapter Nine

My memory is a jumble as to the exact sequence of what happened over the next three years. There are so few photos to remind me of dates. In fact, of any of us taken between when my grandmother died and when I was old enough to purchase a small Kodak Instamatic camera of my own. There was just so much happening over those years between when I was nine and twelve, events that changed all our lives.

The one thing that did not change though was my father's attitude towards me. If I had thought my grandfather living in the house would curtail his night-time activities, I was very much mistaken. His sneaking into my bedroom continued, as did the beatings. Andy and I did gather up enough courage to protest about sharing bathtimes, an argument we won, thanks to my brother's inventiveness.

'We are too big to bath together,' we protested. 'Anyhow, aren't we old enough now to wash ourselves?'

Silence was my father's answer to that.

'I mean,' Andy continued, not letting himself be intimidated by our father's lack of reaction, 'no one at school has to get in their bath with their sisters.'

Our father did not ask how he knew that – he was far too smart to let Andy see that this remark bothered him. Clearly, he thought there must have been some sort of conversation with other boys at school and he certainly did not want any information about his treatment of us falling into the wrong ears. Remember, this was the eighties not the sixties and teachers were becoming aware of the signs of child abuse to look for.

'Mmm,' said Dad, 'you have a point, son. I'll tell you what, you go first and your sister can go in after you get out. How about that?'

We had no choice but to agree, though it sounded as though he still thought he could supervise my bath.

'Hey, Andy,' I said when we were alone, 'did you really tell your classmates that we bathed together?'

'Of course not, stupid! Hardly want to be laughed at, do I? Just wanted him to believe it,' he said with a grin. 'Let him think we talk. We got our own way, didn't we?'

Well, Andy might have, but not me.

He might have agreed to letting us bathe separately, but that did not stop my father coming in when I was in the bath. Nor did it stop him touching me. The beatings, as I grew older, became worse. I learnt not to cry, just to endure them. He used whatever he could lay his hands on to inflict pain: a cane, a slipper and those heavy hands of his.

'You've been a bad girl,' he would tell me.

Then there were the times I was 'a good girl, his special one, the one he wanted to touch and fondle'. When any other adult innocently praised me and called me 'good', I would force myself not to let a shudder run through my body.

*

Those early years at school I actually have little recollection of. I know I was allowed to go to a few birthday parties, where the friendly parents' aim was to make sure every child enjoyed themselves. We were fed sandwiches, cakes and ice cream as well as being encouraged to play games and make as much noise as we wanted, something I was hardly used to. I would wonder, each time a father was present, if they too touched their daughters in those places that now I considered private. Something I wanted to ask, but I never did. Some sixth sense told me that they would turn away from me if I said those words.

And what about my relationship with my mother? It became, if anything, cooler. I was only too aware that whatever affection she had for her children was channelled solely in Andy's direction and there was none left over for Gavin or me.

I felt her watching me, gauging my reaction to her indifference. Even worse, I began to suspect that she was trying to put a wedge between Andy and me. When the two of us sat chatting or playing a game, it never took her long to interrupt and try to divert his attention away from me to her or to ask him to fetch something for her.

Anything, I thought, to get him away from me.

Sadly, though, I loved her still. The bond formed before we enter this world appears to be an unbreakable one and the child I was then was incapable of breaking it. Instead, each day I still hoped for her to show me some affection.

When I lay in my bed, I wanted her to come in, sit near me and read me a story.

'You are old enough to choose your own books and read them for yourself,' was her answer when I asked if she would read me one of my favourites, like she had done when we were younger.

She did, however, keep to her routine of coming up to say goodnight to us. 'Time for lights out, Lynn,' she would say from the doorway and then she was gone. But I would still hear her in Andy's room, chatting away to him for what seemed like ages.

I would strain my ears to hear what was being said and was convinced I heard her kissing him goodnight, something she never did with me. In fact, the only time it was just the two of us was when my nails needed cutting or my hair needed brushing. More than once I tried to give her a hug. Not that she ever responded. Instead, she would just stand with her arms tightly down at her sides, stiff and unyielding, or even worse, give me a gentle push and say, 'Run along now, Lynn, you're not a baby anymore.'

No, I wasn't, but I was still a child – *her* child.

There was one time a memory I still cling to; when after cutting my nails I simply said, 'I love you, Mummy.'

'I know you do, Lynn,' and I heard her sigh. When I drew on my courage to raise my head and look into her eyes, I saw not impatience, but sadness. She hugged me gently then.

'Time for bed, Lynn.'

For once, I did not scuttle away.

'Do you love Andy more than me?' I blurted out. A question I already knew the answer to, but I just wanted to hear her say no.

'It's not that, Lynn. It's that he needs me more than you,' was her answer. And I so wanted to say that I needed her too.

'You're your daddy's favourite, though. He doesn't hide that, does he? And that is why I spend a little more time with your brother.'

I was too young then to understand just how many of my unspoken questions she answered that evening.

It was not long after my grandfather had moved in with us that my mother began to change. She, who never went out of the house or had visitors with a hair out of place, began to take less care of her appearance. Her hair was just scraped back, her face often bare of make-up and high heels seemed a thing of the past. Not only that, she had begun to wear glasses, which my father told her crossly did not suit her.

'Well, if you must! Keep them for the house, there's no reason to wear them out.'

He almost threw some money at her one morning when I was leaving for school: 'For God's sake, Kathy, get yourself into the hairdresser's.'

Those impatient comments, however, failed to have the effect they would once have done. In fact, her disinterest in his opinion of her just seemed to increase. Instead of spending hours in the kitchen preparing food that she knew he liked, she just served up hastily prepared meals.

This was something else that my father noticed and grumbled about.

'I don't know what you do all day,' he would say, pushing the food round his plate.

'I'm tired, John,' was her answer, one that gained her no sympathy. 'There's a lot to do in this house.'

'You're always tired, Kathy. Get the children to help you more, they're old enough.'

And we did try, but nothing we did ever seemed right to her. If we vacuumed, we had overlooked a strip of the carpet; when we washed up, we left grease stains or the glasses were smeary. She looked for fault and almost seemed to cheer up when she found it. Even so, the slightest little thing upset her. More than once I saw tears in her eyes, something I had never seen before. I know now that, as well as being worried about her health, she was severely depressed.

She needed glasses because she had the beginnings of cataracts. 'That's what old people have, isn't it?' I heard her say angrily when she was on the phone to her mother. 'Not someone my age. The optician must have got it wrong.'

Then there were the regular hospital visits. She never said why she was going, so even now I don't know what her problem was then. But all three of us could see there was something wrong.

We also noticed that her attitude towards Gavin changed around then. When my father was away on business, she started being much nicer to him. And he in his turn, I could see, had put aside his anger towards her. I sensed something else; it showed in the odd glance he gave her: he knew something Andy and I did not and it concerned him. Most of her conversation directed towards Gavin consisted of requests, 'Can you fetch that for me' or 'Gavin, would you go to the shops, I'm just worn out' or 'Could you help with the supper' was not unusual, but the 'Thank you' and a warm smile afterwards certainly was.

My father's temper seemed, if anything, worse during those weeks. Each time he left for work or even better, one of his trips, we all – including, I suspect, my grandfather – breathed a sigh of relief. My mother gave no sign that she missed him.

It was during that time that my father's attention turned to Andy.

He had only been away for two days. Gavin had helped our mother prepare a meal. Dad actually thanked her, told her she was looking better and complimented her on a dress she was wearing. With this change in the atmosphere, we all relaxed slightly, although I was dreading bedtime. Would he leave me alone, I wondered, stay downstairs with my mother or not?

To my relief, my father just looked up from where he was sitting, told me to go upstairs and get ready for bed. 'You have the first bath, Lynn,' he told me. 'Then you can spend some time reading that book you've been looking at.'

I sponged and washed myself as quickly as I could and was in my pyjamas and out of there within minutes.

'Andy,' I called out, 'your turn!' and then climbed into bed and picked up my book. I was lost in the pages when I heard the footsteps. I froze: it was him coming up the stairs. 'No,' I said to myself, 'please no! Don't let him come in here.' He didn't; instead I heard the handle of the bathroom door being turned and I knew he had gone inside.

'Why?' I asked myself, but deep down, I knew. I crept out of bed, tiptoed over to the bathroom door and leant against the wall. What was happening behind that door? But I didn't have any thoughts as to what I would do if I heard what I was almost expecting to. At first, I could not hear either of them talking, just the sound of water splashing. He's not doing anything, I decided, and started to creep away. I certainly did not want him coming out and catching me spying on him. It was then I heard that one word coming out of my brother's mouth.

'No!'

'Don't be silly, Andy.'

It was my father's voice.

'No!'

And then came a sound I knew only too well, the sound of a hand hitting bare, wet flesh. I wanted to open that door, shout at my father to leave my brother alone, but my courage deserted me as it had the first time he spanked me.

That night, it was me who crept into my brother's room.

'Did he hurt you?' I asked.

'Yes,' said Andy. But no more was forthcoming as he turned so his back was to me. He wrapped his arms around his legs and curled up as tightly as possible. It was the same way I lay after our father had touched me in between my legs. I knew then that he had done something bad to Andy and whatever it was, it had made my brother feel ashamed.

For the next few days my father did not come near me, nor did he go into the bathroom when Andy was there. I think my brother began to believe that whatever had happened was just a one-off. If he had believed that, a few days later he was proved wrong. I heard my father go into the bathroom and heard my brother shout 'No!', then silence. I knew what that meant: my father's hand was clamped over my brother's mouth.

This time, Andy told me what had happened.

'It was horrible,' he said. 'He kept touching my willie when I was in the bath. He squeezed it and it really hurt. Then he hit me when I tried to wriggle away. He told me that is what fathers and sons do together. I don't believe him, do you?'

'No, I don't. He's been doing that to me for years, he told me not to talk about it. So if it's what all fathers do, why does it have to be a secret?'

Noticing the tears trickling down my cheeks, Andy placed an arm around my shoulders and I saw that he was crying as well.

'He did something worse than that,' he said, after his tears had stopped long enough for him to talk.

'What?'

'He tried to make me bend over the bath, he wanted to stick his willie in me. He hurt me then. Really hurt me, Lynn. Is that what he's been doing to you?'

'No, he uses his hands. He puts them all over me and he uses his fingers too. I hate it. And he beats me. You know that, don't you? He says I've been bad, but I'm not, am I?'

I started crying again and Andy hugged me.

'When I'm big enough, I'll beat him,' my brother said fiercely, clenching his fists.

That was the night all love for our father left my brother, leaving something in its place that festered inside him for most of his life.

'I told him, I told him that I hated him. That I was going to tell Mum on him. He hit me again then. Said there would be more where that came from, if I started bothering my mother, or running around telling stories about our family. And I needn't think of going to Grandpa either. He wouldn't listen to anything bad about him, he would just stop loving me. But I don't care what he says. I'm going to tell Mum, she'll stop him.'

When I heard the faith he still had in her I felt even sadder. I wanted to tell him that I believed our mother knew everything our father got up to. That it was he, not us, who was important to her and that she would do almost anything to keep her marriage safe. I hoped I was wrong – after all, she loved Andy much more than she did me – so just maybe she would listen to him and tell our father to stop.

I went back to my room then and lay awake, wondering what the morning would bring.

No sooner had I opened my eyes than Andy came in.

'I'm not waiting for us to be called down,' he said, 'I know she's up and as soon as he leaves for work, I'm going down there. I want to catch her before Grandpa gets up. She'll listen to me, I know she will.'

He perched on my bed as we waited for the sound of the front door opening and shutting behind our father. However tough he was trying to act, my brother was nervous – I could feel his legs trembling through my bedclothes.

Nervous or not, as soon as we heard that front door open and slam shut, Andy was off my bed.

'Right, I'm going now,' he said as he squared his shoulders and marched down the stairs, all ready to confront our mother.

He was back in less than five minutes.

'And?'

'She told me she had another hospital appointment,' he said somewhat shamefaced. 'Her eyes are sore again. Then she asked me what it was I wanted, but what could I say? She seemed really upset about going back to the hospital. Anyhow, I thought I would wait till she's feeling better and then talk to her.'

He won't, I thought, but didn't say so. He had summoned up just enough courage once but I doubted he would be able to do it twice – I just knew from his expression that his nerve had gone.

My father must also have shared that opinion and gloated over it. He now had two compliant children whom he could control. His next move was made on me, not my brother. Even so, in a way it punished Andy. He would have heard him slipping into my room. Now he knew just what he was capable of. He must have lain in his bed imagining what was happening to me behind my bedroom door. As my older brother, he believed that he should be able to protect his little sister. And now, by not telling our mother, he felt he had messed up badly, for failure to do so showed him to be weak. This, I think, was always what he had believed and what was to cause him so many issues in the future.

'Your mother's fallen asleep,' my father told me that night with the knowing smirk I had grown to detest. 'And I need a little company, don't I, so who other than from my favourite girl, eh?'

I wanted to tell him to go away, that I wanted to sleep. Instead, my fingers just clutched the bedclothes as I looked up at him without saying a word.

Over the years I had learnt to switch myself off from feeling anything when he molested me. Just lie there like a wooden doll, show no reaction. Let him do what he has to do. And don't give him the satisfaction of allowing one whimper or plea to leave your mouth, were my mantras. My father must have thought I had become wise to building those little walls to protect myself, ones that he was determined to take down. He did not want a wooden impassive doll, he wanted a frightened little girl in that bed.

Instead of pulling back the sheet as I had expected, he pulled me half out of bed so I was lying with my feet dangling down. I could feel his breath on my back as he leant over me and swiftly pulled down my pyjama bottoms and pushed the top up around my neck. This time he spread my legs and pulled a pillow under my stomach before sliding his finger inside me. I forgot my resolve not to cry at both the indignity and the pain. That feeling of helplessness was too strong for me not to show any emotion. He, feeling the sobs rising in my throat, held my head down in the bedclothes to muffle them.

Then he was gone, but not before telling me, 'You needn't run to your grandpa with your stories. Be worse for you and your brother if you do. Mind you, he's not got the guts, has he?' And he left me there.

Why I did not go to my grandfather is a question I have asked myself time and again. Or even my English grandmother. I have searched for the answer. Why? Why do children keep quiet about something so terrible happening to them? There were people Andy and I could have gone to for help. I suppose part of the answer is that although children might disobey their parents on little things, they can't bring themselves to do so on bigger ones. That fear of what might happen if we talk is so deeply embedded in us that we almost never do. Not only that, for mixed with that fear is another word: shame.

My brother though was braver than I had given him credit for. It's something I have learnt: we can be made angrier by seeing someone we love being hurt than when we ourselves are.

And I was right: Andy had been awake when my father slipped into my room. He had heard my muffled sobs and it was that which reignited his determination to talk to our mother.

He waited until the weekend to tackle her. We knew that Dad was taking our grandpa to a football match.

'I'm going to talk to her once they are out of the house,' he told me, giving my hand a squeeze. 'Mum will sort him out. Perhaps she will throw him out. That would be nice, wouldn't it? Anyhow, whatever she does, she'll make it alright, Lynn,' he told me solemnly with such trust shining in his eyes.

For until he went to her that Saturday, he totally believed that all mothers are there to make everything alright. But this was not a scabbed knee she could put a dressing on or a ripped article of clothing she could mend. This was not, I was certain, something she would want to hear. At the ages we were then, neither Andy nor I knew that what my father was doing was illegal. We did not realise that if his crime were discovered, he would go to prison and some of that disgrace would be smeared onto her. She would never be able to hold her head up in public again. Had we known all that, we would have had a threat to hold over them both. But then we didn't: we believed our parents owned us and only they could dictate how we were treated. That did not stop me hoping, just a little bit, that she would stand up for us. A hope that was extinguished the moment my brother returned upstairs. One look at his drooping shoulders and white face told me he was shattered, that his faith in our mother, like my hope, had vanished. He was no longer my protector but a little boy who no longer knew who he could turn to.

Now it was my turn to be the strong one and, stretching out my arm, I took his hand in mine and gently pulled him towards me.

'Tell me about it,' I said, 'what did you say to her?'

'That he touched me here,' he told me, pointing to his crotch, 'and he rubbed his willie against me.'

'And what did she say?'

'Nothing at first, her eyes sort of darkened. And then,' he gulped and I could see that tears were not very far away, 'she told me to go to my room. That was after I told her that he did even worse things to you. And do you know what she said then? She told me I shouldn't talk dirty, not if I wanted her to keep on loving me.'

My mother had carefully put into words a child's greatest fear: it's not being beaten or being abused, it's being unloved. For that bond that ties us to our mothers is formed when we are still in the womb. The thought of not being the centre of her universe can be too much to bear, as I know now it was for both my brothers.

That day, she must have been aware of it too.

Chapter Ten

It was while browsing the Web that I came across the site named 'Heroic Mothers' – mothers who, when their children were in danger, ran into burning buildings, stood in front of a charging puma or dived into a stormy sea.

Mothers would, it seemed, put their own lives at risk for their children.

It was in the nature of the female, be it animal or human.

I clicked on photo after photo of those smiling heroic women as they held a child whose life was more precious than their own.

But I didn't need a photo to bring up the memory of what mine did when confronted by my brother. If she tackled my father, I never heard about it. She certainly never questioned me. I can only assume what she did was absolutely nothing. Apart from packing a bag and going to visit her mother, that is, and she never even told us she was going. She left it to our grandfather to inform us that she had gone and would be away for a week or two.

Had I really hoped that she would do more? In my imagination had I pictured her running up those stairs, taking me in her arms and saying everything was going to be alright? That she had not known what he did, that she was going to make sure he never hurt us again?

I can't remember if I did. For I think I had already learnt that there is a big difference between hope and belief.

And my brother, what did he think would happen that day?

Sadly, up until then he had complete faith in her love for him. That she, when she heard the truth, would turn into a fierce protector of her beloved offspring. And the effect that disillusion had on him?

That, I still find difficult to think about.

It was my grandfather who cooked us an early supper the day she left. Neither of our parents were to be seen. I thought that maybe my mother was in her bedroom; my father was out.

'What have you two done to upset your mother?' Grandpa asked.

Looking into his kindly eyes, there was a split second when I wanted to tell him. Even then, I sensed he would not want to hear any stories about his son, the only child he had with his beloved late wife. The man who had put his needs first when he provided him with a home once he was a widower. My grandfather must have known that his son had done that against his wife's wishes. Then I had no idea that there might have been another reason why he would take his son's side.

All those thoughts running through my head must have been going through my brother's too, for we caught each other's eye and in unison said, 'Don't know.'

'Well, she's taken off and gone to visit her mother. She told me she needed a break from her family. Asked me to keep an eye on you all and get your supper.'

'How long has she gone for?' Andy asked.

'She didn't say,' he replied. 'Until she feels like coming back, I suppose.'

Nothing more was said about my mother's going. Grandpa microwaved some chicken nuggets, said laughingly that he would have to start practising cooking more and told us he would like us to get ourselves ready for bed.

'I know it's early,' he said, 'but I need to have a chat with your dad when he comes back, which,' he added, glancing at his watch, 'will not be much longer. So, take your books upstairs and amuse yourselves and I'll see you in the morning, alright?'

We agreed and, relieved we would not have to face our father, Andy and I scuttled up the stairs as fast as our legs would carry us.

Andy and I were thoroughly shaken. Thoughts of what was going to happen to us were spinning around in our heads. What was our father going to do to us now, we asked each other, and why had our mother taken off like that?

'I mean,' said Andy, 'she didn't even say goodbye.'

Then we heard our father's car turn into the drive and both fell silent.

We heard our grandfather talking to him in the hall and their footsteps as they went into the lounge and the door was closed.

I wished then that we could hear what they were talking about and I wish now that I had summoned up the courage to have crept down those stairs and listened. Because to this day I still don't know what my mother told him when she left or anything about the conversation my grandfather had with his son, though from what I have subsequently learnt, I can hazard a guess.

My mother was gone for a week – a week when everything became much worse. A time when what took place made Andy and me realise there would be no help coming our way.

Our father tackled us the next evening. Again, Grandpa gave us an early supper and told us to take ourselves off to our rooms.

'I know your father wants a chat with you both. He'll come up and see you when he gets in.'

That was two hours after we had eaten and both of us were almost sick with fear. What was going to happen now, we asked each other, knowing whatever it was would not be good.

We were in my room when he appeared. There were no hellos, just a silent, stern-faced man who sat on my bed, told us to stand in front of him while he spelt out what would happen to us if we ever tried to cause him trouble again.

'Your mother and I love each other and there's nothing that will come between us. Nothing! So, I want you to listen carefully. If you do anything like this again or attempt to damage our family, it will be you two who will suffer, not your mother or me. Do you understand?' His tone was not angry but so cold that we knew whatever was coming next would not be idle threats.

'So, don't ever try and upset her again. Have I your word on that?'

We nodded, hoping that was the end of his lecture – it wasn't.

'Good. Because now I'm going to explain just what will happen if either of you break your word on that. You won't be punished by a beating or being sent to your room because I would consider you no longer want to be part of our family so other arrangements would be made for you. You would be taken to a children's home and there you would stay until you left school. Oh, and just in case you think you would be at the same one, you wouldn't. Andy would be placed in a boys' home and you, Lynn, would go to a girls-only place. So, not only would you not be seeing your mother and me, you would not be seeing each other for a long time. Now do you understand?'

We managed to stutter out a 'yes' before the tears began to run down our faces. And then, as we both stood there, he changed completely.

'Oh, come here, you two! You know I love you,' and Andy was pulled onto his lap for a cuddle while I leant against him as his arm snaked around my shoulders. 'Now everything is going to be alright, we'll say nothing more about it. I'll send out for a pizza, so stop your tears now. I'm sure you can have a bit more supper, Grandpa says you haven't had much.'

And with those few sentences he changed from persecutor to protector.

'Just understand that what goes on in this home stays private. And no more upsetting your mother and we'll all be just fine, won't we?'

And we, so happy to see that nice Father had returned, like small puppets nodded our heads while he, the well-rehearsed manipulator, expertly pulled the strings.

That evening, true to his word, pizzas were ordered. My father piled plates onto the kitchen table and told us to tuck in. All of us, including Gavin, joined our father and grandfather in the lounge to eat pizza and watch television.

It was when the Nine O'Clock News came on that my father exclaimed, 'Goodness, is that the time? You lot better get yourselves off to bed.'

Goodnight hugs were given, our hair was ruffled by Grandpa and in a slight daze, Andy and I took ourselves off up the stairs.

Was that it, I asked myself, had everything changed?

There were no footsteps on the stairs that evening and, curled up in my bed, I allowed myself to believe with a child's naivety that maybe nothing was going to happen again.

It took my father two days before he showed me who was in charge. He was so certain neither Andy nor I would ever talk that the moment he entered my room, he made it clear what he wanted.

This time there were no cuddles or whispered words telling me I was special – he had no intention of wasting time on those. The child I was did not know the word for what happened. The adult does: it was rape, brutal rape. There is no other word that would lessen what it was. He did it to me that night. There might have been attempts to wipe it from my memory, attempts that actually succeeded for a while, but deep down I always knew what happened and that is very clear to me now.

I was woken by a hand over my mouth, the other one yanking my pyjama bottoms down, and then before I had a chance to wriggle away, his weight was crushing the air out of my lungs. There was pain, hot searing pain, spreading through my body as he thrust that thing inside of me. I could still hear his grunting through the pain. The last thrust was even harder. He yelled in triumph and stars danced in front of my eyes, then there was blackness, soft enfolding blackness.

I came to, hearing his voice.

'Wake up, Lynn,' he was saying, 'wake up!'

Opening my eyes, I saw my father sitting beside me.

'Say something, Lynn,' he kept repeating. 'Tell me you are alright.' But I could not speak. There was a dull throbbing pain between my legs. I did not understand what it was, only that it was there. Slowly, I moved my hand down and felt something warm and sticky. As I lifted it out of the covers, I saw my fingers were bright red.

I wanted to scream, I knew it was blood. Tiny drops of it glistened as they slid from my fingers and landed on my sheet.

My father saw it too and I could see that although he was pretending that there was nothing there, he was panicked.

'Oh, Lynn,' he said, 'what have you done? Just stay there. Don't move, I'll be back in a moment.' His hand touched my face gently and I saw both concern and fright in his eyes. 'You're going to be alright. Just stay in your bed, don't try and move. Alright?'

Panic at the state I was in must have given his feet wings for I heard him flying down those stairs. There was only one person in the house he could talk to – his father. Then I had no idea what it was he said to him, but now I do.

My father need not have told me not to move, I was too frightened to do so. As I lay wondering what was going on downstairs, I wanted my mother, wanted to call out to Andy.

Somehow, I felt if I did, it would make everything much worse. I was so scared that I could not bring myself to touch that sore place again. I could not bear the thought of seeing my fingers red with blood. Did bleeding down there mean I was dying? I kept asking myself, my little girl's worries circling in my head, and through the haze came the murmur of voices, two sets of footsteps, and then my grandfather came into the room.

'You've had a wee accident, Lynn darling,' he told me. 'You fell out of bed. You must have been having a nasty dream. What was it, a monster trying to carry you off?'

Not that he wanted an answer to his questions. He was, I came to realise many years later, just removing the truth from my mind and replacing it with something much more acceptable.

'Now, Lynn, your dad's told me that your stomach hurts so I've brought you up something to make it better. Not come from gypsy stock for nothing,' he added with a wink. 'We've got magic potions that can fix everything and anything. And this one is especially for little girls' stomachs. Here, let me help you sit up.'

His arm went around my shoulders, pillows were plumped before a mug containing dark brown liquid was held to my lips.

'I know it smells nasty,' he said, 'but if you just swallow it in one go, it won't taste too bad.'

Obediently, I gulped down the bitter liquid.

'Good girl, Lynn. Now here's some warm milk to take the taste away. I've stirred in some honey, just the way you like it.' And he held a second mug to my lips.

'You'll be right as rain in the morning,' were the last words I heard before I fell into a deep sleep.

I don't think I even finished my milk.

When I finally woke my grandfather was sitting in the chair by my bed.

'How you feeling now, Lynn?' he asked as soon as my eyes swivelled round to meet his.

I did not answer him for my head felt fuzzy as flashes of what had happened the night before began to trickle into my memory.

'Oh well, you need to wake up properly, I can see you're still sleepy. You had a bit of an accident last night. Doubt if you remember much about it.'

He was wrong – I did. Or at least I thought I did. My head was still woozy and I was having difficulty focusing my thoughts. Was that heavy weight pressing all the air out of me a dream or had it really happened? And the pain that tore through my body, the blood that dripped from my fingers, surely I had not dreamt it?

My grandfather must have sensed what was going on in my mind for he cut across my thoughts. His large hand swallowed my small one.

'Now, don't fret, Lynn. Whatever it was you were dreaming about frightened you so much you fell out of bed. Well, judging by the thwack you made, you must have jumped from it. Your father heard the thump and rushed up here. You had to be lifted back in. He's been very worried, you managed to knock yourself out.'

I must have looked at him unbelievingly for he continued, 'You don't remember that? Well, you did hit your head hard when you fell. Now you are going to stay in bed today, let that head of yours get better. I'll tell your dad you are awake when I go down and make you some breakfast. Nice scrambled eggs alright for you?'

Although everything he was saying to me was in his cheerful voice, I could see how tired he was. His forehead was deeply furrowed and his eyes told me he was worried. He looks old, I thought, but more than that, distracted by something that was worrying him.

Was I hurt more than he had told me?

'I want to go to the lavatory,' I said, moving to swing my legs out of the bed.

'Careful now, darling, I'll help you,' and strong arms lifted me.

Once I was sitting on the lavatory I dared myself to look down to that spot between my legs. There was no blood, not there and not on my pyjamas either. Nor when I climbed back into bed was there any on the sheets so my grandfather must have been telling me the truth, I reasoned.

At that age I could not imagine that two men might, after making sure I would not wake up, have used a washing machine and tumble dryer to wash away any evidence. Without those telltale blood-stained sheets, I would have to believe the story that was fed me.

My grandfather not only made my breakfast, but carried it into my room.

'Eat this all up,' he told me, sitting on the end of the bed. 'Then you can have another of my magic potions. You'll soon be up and about.'

No sooner had I eaten my breakfast than I was given some more of my grandfather's remedy. Within seconds, my eyes shut and I slid into a deep, dreamless sleep.

The sun was streaming through my window when I woke for the second time. My grandfather was right, the pain had almost disappeared. There was just a faint ache. This time I was alone and needing to get to the lavatory again. As I swung my legs out of the bed and stood up, I felt a little shaky, but then I was still a little sleepy too.

My father must have been listening for any movement from my room for the moment I went back to it, I heard him bounding up the stairs.

'You're up, Lynn. How do you feel now? Oh, you did give us such a fright,' he kept repeating as he followed me into my room, where I climbed back into the cocoon of my bedding.

Looking up into his face, I saw nothing but concern in his expression.

I felt even more bewildered now. Hadn't he hurt me and made me bleed, or had it been as my grandfather said, a bad dream? If confusion showed in my face then my father chose to ignore it.

'You don't remember what happened, do you, Lynn?'

I shook my head. Using my voice was still proving difficult. Words seemed to have stuck firmly in my throat. What I wanted then was for another of Grandpa's magic potions to send me straight back to sleep again.

'Oh, I think you are still in shock,' he said, 'I know you had a very bad nightmare. I heard you scream and came up the stairs. I was too late though, you had already thrown yourself out of the bed. The thud you made, well, I was frightened you had broken something. But you don't even remember me picking you up, do you?'

'No,' I managed to say.

'And when I got you back in bed, you kept muttering under your breath that there was a monster in your room. It was big, you said, and it was going to attack you again. It was certainly a nasty fall. That's when I fetched your grandfather, he knew what to do better than me. Anyhow, the good news is that we are keeping you home for a couple of days. Make sure you are completely well before you go back to school. Got to make sure my girl is fully recovered, haven't I?'

His words both comforted and confused me. I wanted to believe what they had told me and that wanting in the end made me accept their version of what happened that night. Even so, that did not stop me wondering why the place between my legs was still so tender. It was that part that still ached, not my head. After all, they had told me that I had banged it badly, so why was there no pain there?

'Come, Lynn, you are still looking pale. You'd better stay in bed. Your grandfather will come up to keep you company. I'm going to fetch Andy from school soon and he'll want to see you. Poor little chap's been very worried, all that commotion woke him up alright.'

And once more my bedding was straightened and my pillows plumped up before he leant down and kissed the top of my head.

'Be back soon,' he promised with a cheery smile as he left me there.

*

Later, when Andy returned from school, he came into my room carrying a bar of chocolate.

'Grandpa told me to give you this,' he said as he pushed it into my hand.

'So, what happened?' he asked. 'Did Dad hurt you again?'

'He said I fell out of bed,' I replied, an answer that made my brother give me a very sceptical look.

'Yes, that's what he told me too. And Grandpa said the same. But is that the truth, Lynn? I thought I heard him come into your room long before he raced down the stairs and I never heard you falling out of bed.'

'Well, it must be, mustn't it? I mean, Grandpa says he heard me as well. Perhaps you were asleep.'

'Maybe,' he replied, but I could hear the doubt in his voice.

And his doubt made something crawl under my skin: the picture of a dark shape lying on me filled my mind. Again, I felt the choking feeling of not being able to breathe and then behind my lids, I saw a face mottled red with glazed eyes that were not even looking down at me. As those memories darted around my head, I knew the truth: I had not fallen out of bed. And as the realisation hit me, I felt bubbles of panic entering my blood.

No, I told myself, it was a dream. For if it wasn't true, it was not only my father who had lied to me, but Grandpa too. And that thought was too much for my young mind to cope with.

'That's what must have happened, Andy,' I said as firmly as I could.

But it was not my brother I wanted to convince that day, it was me.

*

It was after what my father and grandfather called 'my accident' that the nightmares worsened. In my dreams there was a dark heavy weight pressing me down; I knew it was going to try to rip my insides out. A scream would force its way out of my throat, making my eyes fly open and forcing me mercifully awake.

It was then that my fear of the dark really began.

A week went by where I was spoilt and cosseted. My father acted the part of the caring father well. And then my mother returned.

Would our lives be better now? I asked myself, hopefully.

They weren't.

Part Two
After

Chapter Eleven

It was about a year after my grandfather's arrival when it became obvious that there was a lot more wrong with my mother than her having cataracts and being tired. No longer did my father complain about her not looking after herself properly. He made no comment at all when she sat at the dining-room table without any make-up, or that she never wore high heels. Now it was he who ran after her, bringing little presents he thought she would like – a pretty scarf, a box of chocolates, bottles of fragrant body lotion and bubble bath – the small luxuries that she had once loved. When he gave them to her, she seemed to have to force a wan smile of thanks, though. Not only that, it was he and my grandfather who took over all of the cooking. This was something that my father had always considered my mother's job. Luckily for us, Grandpa turned out to be quite good at it.

'It was always something I liked doing, but back in my day, men weren't supposed to even set foot in the kitchen – women's work, it was. And any boy who wanted to be a chef was called a poof. Times have changed alright,' he declared, for the night before he was glued to the television, watching a young male chef cook amazing food. The following morning, he placed perfect omelettes on our plates for breakfast. Dusty cookery books were taken down from the bookshelves for him and my father to pore over; every night it seemed a new dish appeared on the table.

My grandfather blossomed; he had found a new interest. And surprisingly, it was one my father appeared to share. Or maybe it was just something that helped take his mind off my mother's illness.

He was spending much more time at home and there were no more overseas trips either. Instead, he stayed working nearby and took time off to accompany my mother to the hospital. Even better for me was that for a while he showed no interest in coming into my bedroom or even supervising our bathtimes. The times of us having to go upstairs became more flexible, especially as we were helping Gavin with the washing-up. We were just thanked for helping, said goodnight to and left to put ourselves to bed.

Under any other circumstances those months would have been happy ones. Gavin had put aside his resentment of Andy and me. Although it was he who took charge of the housework, he was good-natured enough to give us small tasks to do that were within our capabilities. But underneath the show of cheerfulness that the adults tried to present to us, we could sense both the strain they were under and their worry. It was also reflected in Gavin's face: he had known all along that whatever was wrong with our mother was far more serious than trouble with her eyes.

It was not until we were told that she had to go into hospital for an operation that we came to understand that too. Never having been, either for a visit or a stay in one, we believed those large grey buildings were where we were taken when we were very ill. One of my parents' friends had been rushed to hospital from his workplace. All we knew was what we overheard: that it was a heart attack and that he had died. 'Roger was so young,' I heard my mother saying, 'he was only in his forties. And God knows what will happen to his family now.' That was when we learnt that it was not only old people who died and hearing that was where our mother was going was very scary for Andy and me.

My father was taking her. We stood in the hall, watching them both come down the stairs. He was carrying her case and she was trying her best to give us a cheerful smile. She gave all three of us a brief hug, said, 'Bye now, be good,' and before we could say anything in return, she was out the door and in the car.

'How long is she going to be in there?' I asked my grandfather.

He paused a little, searching for the answer that would satisfy us.

'Didn't she tell you?' prompted Andy.

'Yes, she said she would only be gone for a few days so don't worry, you two. Your father will be at the hospital with her quite a bit, so Gavin and I will look after you both.'

'Why's she going in? Is it her eyes again?' Andy said with a puzzled frown.

'No, bairns, not this time. She's got a problem with her stomach, nothing serious. She'll be back in a day or two.'

'But what's wrong with her?' we asked in unison.

'It's nothing for you two to worry about. She'll be back right as rain, see if she isn't.'

And with that he started talking about something different.

Grown-ups, Andy and I decided as we talked together, are not very good at lying to children. But Gavin was not quite a grown-up and it was he who we went to the following day.

'You know what's really wrong with her, don't you?' we asked when we cornered him at the top of the stairs. 'You've been to the hospital to visit her, haven't you?'

For once, rather to our surprise, he did not tell us to go away. Instead, he just told us to go into my room and he would come in and talk to us there.

When he came in, we could see just how upset he was and that worried us even more.

'She won't be back in a couple of days,' he explained, 'I don't know why Grandpa told you that.'

'How long then?'

'A couple of weeks, I guess.'

'Please, Gavin, can you tell us what's really wrong with her? I'm fed up with them saying we are too young to know anything, she's our mother too,' I pleaded.

'She's got a lump inside her that has to be removed,' he told us. 'If they leave it there, it will just get bigger and bigger and that's not good.'

'So,' asked Andy, 'is that why she's been going to the hospital so much?'

'Yes, ever since they found out the lump was cancer,' he explained with a very serious expression on his face. 'They caught it early. And she's been going to the hospital for radiation.'

'What's that?'

'It's a treatment that makes the lump get smaller until it disappears. Well, that's what I've been told anyhow,' he said.

'And why didn't it work?'

'It did for a while, I think. All I really know is that they have to take it out now.'

Gavin knew that two children of our ages were unlikely to have much understanding of either cancer or radiation, but he could certainly see just how frightened we were and tried to explain it all as simply as possible. For that, Andy and I were grateful. After all, she was his mother too and however much he tried to hide it, he was just as frightened as we were.

'So, if it didn't go away, why didn't she just keep going?' asked a puzzled Andy. I saw by the slump in his shoulders that it was beginning to sink in that our mother was really very ill.

'I'm really not sure,' answered Gavin, 'I've only been told so much. It's like no one wants to talk about it. I think it did at first and then it's come back somewhere else. That's what Grandpa explained to me, anyhow.'

'Why didn't he tell us too?' I asked indignantly.

'He thought you were both too young to understand everything so promise me you won't tell him I've told you.'

'No, we won't,' we chorused.

Without voicing it, all three of us were united in our concerns about our mother.

'So, what are they going to do now?'

And here, our older brother decided it was just too difficult to explain what a hysterectomy was. Instead, he said that they had to take the place out where the cancer had grown.

'That means she won't be able to have any more children,' he told us gravely.

'Well, that doesn't matter, does it?' I said. 'Don't think she wants any more.'

'No,' said Gavin sadly. 'I don't even know if she wants the ones she has.'

And as we sat in that room, it was the first time we felt a bond form between us. All three of us might have loved her in different ways, but we each felt that she had never really been there for us, not when it mattered at least.

'And then she'll come home, Gavin?' asked Andy and I could tell he was having trouble digesting all of the information he had been given. Both of us had worked out that if the grown-ups had not told us anything there was a reason – and that must be that our mother was far sicker than we had been led to believe.

'Yes, Andy, as soon as she's recovered from the operation, she will come home.'

Thinking of the time of my mother's decline always makes me feel sad. Even now, I'm not sure why she had so many hospital visits. I can only assume that when the cancer was first diagnosed, it was in a different part of her and the radiation did work on that particular one. I'm not even sure how much my father knew. I can only assume she did not tell him straight away. Perhaps she thought that keeping it quiet would stop it being real.

If anything positive came of that whole miserable period, it was the time the little shoots of my friendship with Gavin were planted. It was a couple of days after the operation, which we had been told was successful, when he knocked on my door and asked if he could come in. He had been to the hospital, he told me, and then he went for a walk. His eyes were red and puffy from crying.

'What is it, Gavin?' I asked, sick with apprehension.

Had something terrible happened? Was she dead?

'She just looks so small in that bed,' he said.

A tear dropped and he brushed it away.

'But was she looking alright?'

'About the same, but she did seem pleased to see me, though. Not that your dad was. You know, he's tried to stop me visiting, but he can't. Only Mum can do that and she doesn't want to. But he hovers, won't give us one minute alone together. And I only want to say that I miss her and want her back home, that we all do.'

His eyes filled again.

'You know what he said to me, just yesterday, that once my mother's back, he's going to tell her I'm old enough to stand on my own two feet and should get a place of my own.'

'Come on, Gavin, Mum would never agree to that, nor would Grandpa, so don't take any notice of him. Once she's home, he'll be happy and forget what he said. You must know that it's not just you he's horrible to.'

He lowered his eyes then and I realised by the embarrassed expression on his face that he knew a great deal more than he was letting on.

'I hope you're right. I am old enough now to go, I just don't want to. Mum needs us all.'

I laid a hand on his arm: 'Don't let him get to you.'

'Oh, and Lynn, you won't forget I wasn't supposed to say anything to you, but it's just that I thought you should both know.' His eyes overflowed again as he gulped, 'There's no one else I can talk to. Your dad hates me and your grandfather goes along with anything he says, doesn't he?'

That was when I realised just how lonely Gavin was and for the first time, I stretched out my hand and took his hand in mine.

Chapter Twelve

A couple of weeks after that conversation with Gavin my father brought my mother home. She was even thinner than when she had gone into hospital, I noticed. My grandfather fussed around her, making sure there was a cushion behind her back and a stool for her to put her feet on, before he disappeared into the kitchen to make tea.

'I can hug you both,' she told Andy and me, 'I'm not that weak.'

I pushed aside the thought that this was not something she had done much of before she had gone to hospital.

'Come over here and let me give you both a kiss. I've heard from your father that you have all been a great help around the house – especially you, Gavin,' and her smile included him as well.

Very little seemed to change over the next few months and we resumed our routine at home and at school. My father also resumed working, but seemed reluctant to travel for more than forty-eight hours, Grandpa continued to cook and the three of us dusted, swept, made our beds and washed up. The biggest change was evident in Gavin: there was never a cross word from him directed towards us.

My father kept away from Andy, but not me. Oh, he left it a while before he started coming into my room, though he did not sneak in nearly as often as he had. After all, he hardly wanted to be caught and both my grandfather and Gavin were spending more time around the house. He never repeated the violence that had injured me but still could not bring himself to leave me completely alone. Grandpa continued living in the new flat above the garage, although he still did a lot of the cooking, and my mother seemed more relaxed and contented.

It must have been about a year after she had been discharged that she had her last hospital check-up. This time she and my father came home wreathed in smiles. She had been given the all-clear, she could live a normal life. Her 'illness', as she called the cancer, was gone.

'Well then,' my grandfather said, 'that's good news and all good news deserves a wee celebration. How about I book us all a holiday? How do you feel about another trip to Scotland? We could spend Easter there, the weather will be fairly mild then. It will be my treat. What do you say, Kathy?'

'Why, I'll say yes and thank you very much, Joe,' was her gracious answer.

My grandfather made a few phone calls. A cottage with all mod cons was rented. I could hardly wait for term to end. Nor, I think, could my mother. She seemed different since she had come home, as did my father. He still did not leave me alone, but the beatings had stopped. I began to believe that at least they had ceased for good. Grandpa was in high spirits, planning all the places he wanted to show us. He was clearly happy for his son that his wife was better and excited about returning to the part of the world he loved and which held so many happy memories for him. And his enthusiasm was contagious for even Gavin seemed in better spirits. He was happy too that he had been chosen to travel with Grandpa by train – my father's car was not big enough for all of us since Andy and I had grown, plus we had an extra passenger.

'You can carry your grandfather's case,' Dad told Gavin when Grandpa was not in the room. 'Don't let him try and pick it up, will you?'

'No, Dad,' he replied and a flash of understanding passed between them. I supposed it was because Grandpa was getting old that my father had said that, so I didn't give it another thought.

I can only describe that holiday as peaceful. None of us knew then that it was to be the last family holiday we would ever have. Although there were few photos taken, Gavin did some drawings, which he gave to both Andy and me.

'Thought you might like them,' he said shyly and I smiled back, pleased that the truce between us remained. Not that there was complete trust, but we had one thing in common: however bad a mother like ours had been, we all loved her in our own way and were just happy that she had regained her health. My mother was relaxed, my father attentive towards her and Grandpa, as well as choosing places we could visit, busied himself looking up old friends.

I still have those paintings that Gavin did of some wildlife he spotted and I particularly love a pen-and-ink drawing of our grandfather. Looking at them gives me pleasure because the events that came after that trip have wiped much of that time from my mind. I do know, however, that we were all happy for the two weeks we were there.

A happiness that would soon disappear when we returned home.

The cancer had come back.

She tried so hard to stay with us, tried as hard as she could. Had the doctors told her then that nothing could save her? I think they had. She must have known that the treatment she agreed to have would only prolong her life, it would not cure her. Or had she even told the truth about being free of cancer? She had, I learnt later, insisted on seeing the doctor on her own. I don't know … All I can remember now are the days when she began having chemotherapy.

She had explained it to us that this was a treatment that would kill the cancer cells. What I felt though was that the treatment was not just killing the cancer cells, it was killing her as well.

'No, Lynn, it's making her better,' my grandfather insisted as he tried his best to reassure me. 'She's in good hands at the hospital. They know what they are doing, she'll be alright.'

I believed him because I was still young enough to think that doctors and hospitals always make us better.

It had been seeing her thick blonde hair that she was once so proud of begin to fall out after two weeks of treatment that had sent me to ask questions of him. To begin with, it just looked dull and thinner. Then I noticed that there were little bald patches appearing. Once her hair loss progressed, she never let any of us see her without a scarf or a hat on her head. Still, I could tell by the fact that her forehead appeared so much higher that there was nothing left under her scarf.

The only good thing about my mother's illness was that we became closer. She wanted me bringing her cups of tea and sitting beside her and for two days after each treatment it was me she wanted in her bedroom, not Andy. She needed me to support her when she went to the bathroom; luckily, I was tall for my age and strong. She would lean on me weakly while my arm went around her waist as I helped her to stumble across the bedroom and into the corridor. It was only a few steps, but it took all her effort to make them. She never wanted me to come in – 'I'll manage,' she told me and standing outside, I could hear the sound of her retching and retching. Sounds that made my heart twist for her. I wanted to cry, I could hardly bear seeing what she was putting herself through, but if she could put on a brave face so could I.

'Back to bed then, Mum,' I would say with a smile when the door opened. Deep down, I think I knew although she did not want to leave my father and us, this was to be her last fight.

Finally, the chemo treatment finished.

'I'm going to be alright now,' my mother told us.

She still did not look well, but I crossed my fingers, hoping this time she would be. On 22 July, my twelfth birthday arrived. There was a very quiet celebration. None of us believed that our mother was better and whatever my father knew, he either kept it to himself, or lived in a state of denial. Not only did he not confide in us, to my relief he rarely came near me during that time.

It was only a week after that birthday dinner that my mother's legs began to swell. I have since learnt that this was the beginning of the end: her organs were shutting down. It was Gavin who told me that this time there was no hope.

'She's dying, Lynn,' he said.

'I know,' I told him – I think I must have known all along. 'How long will it take?' I added.

'I don't know,' he said miserably. 'The doctor has told her there's a bed in the hospice.'

'Is that a hospital?'

'No, it's a place where they make sure that you are cared for until the end. But she's said no, she wants to stay here. It's her home, she told him, and that's where her family is. She wants to be with us. The doctor's arranging for a nurse to come, she'll help with the medication. That's all I know, promise.'

In the morning it was me who opened the door to the nurse. She sat me down and explained what it was she had to do: to set up a little machine that would help my mother self-administer the drug that would help with any pain: 'There's medication as well, which I will leave with her,' she told me. She asked if there was anyone else in the house apart from my father and I knew she meant was there another adult there?

'My grandfather, he lives in the flat above the garage,' I told her.

After the nurse was gone I took tea up to my mother and saw what the nurse had brought. It was a horrible little machine, I thought, each time I heard its faint click and knew more of that drug had gone into my mother. For each beep told me that it was there to ease the pain that the thing inside her was causing. Each click also told me that the cancer was quietly sucking the life out of her.

The date my father rang for the ambulance is still imprinted on my mind: 21 August 1982. I was in my room, in that state between half-asleep and half-awake, when I heard his voice shouting for all of us children to get up. There was no mistaking the fear in his voice and I knew that my mother was much worse.

Pulling on our dressing gowns, we stumbled down the stairs. We knew this was going to be bad. Ashen-faced, my father was standing in the hall. He told us he had rung for the ambulance and for us to open the door to them, 'and Gavin,' he added, before rushing back up the stairs, 'get your grandfather.'

We did not need to be told that if an ambulance was on its way it meant she was going to be taken to hospital. We saw the blue light flashing as it turned into the drive. I knew that they only put that on for an emergency.

Confronted by two frightened children, they tried to be as kind as possible, asked us where her room was and then, carrying the stretcher, proceeded up the stairs with Andy and me following them. We stood in the bedroom doorway and watched as they gently moved her from the bed to the stretcher. We saw how a blanket was tucked around her and a small pillow placed under her head. As they bent to pick it up, she managed to say, 'Just wait a moment, please,' and, looking in our direction, beckoned for us to go to her side, where we knelt down, one on each side of her. She was almost too weak to lift her arms, but managed to put one on each of our shoulders.

'Look after each other,' she said, 'and Lynn,' and her hand touched mine, 'I always loved you,' she whispered in my ear, 'I want you to remember that.' Exhausted by that tiny burst of energy, she managed to mumble to no one in particular, 'I'm ready now,' before her eyes closed.

The paramedics picked the stretcher up and carried it down the stairs slowly with us in their wake. Gavin and my grandfather were already waiting in the hall when we all came down.

'Kathy,' I heard Grandpa say and her eyes flickered open, Gavin flew to her side and her hand touched his as she smiled up at him. And then, with my father by her side, she was carried into the ambulance. I watched as they slid the stretcher in. All I could see was the red blanket that covered her tiny form and the silhouette of my father sitting by her side before the doors were closed. The flashing blue light came on, its siren was switched on and within seconds, it had disappeared from sight.

'We will all go to see her tomorrow,' my grandfather said.

It was a journey that was never made.

She died that night.

Chapter Thirteen

It was our grandfather who broke the news to us that our mother had died. The three of us just sat there, too stunned to take in what he had just told us. He added that my father was still at the hospital with my grandmother. It was the doctor there who had phoned him.

As the truth of what he had told us began to sink in, Gavin turned so white I thought he was going to faint, while Andy, his face contorted with grief, screamed that it was not true and ran from the room. I knew the moment he reached his bedroom he would throw himself on the bed and howl out his grief.

And what of me? I know I just couldn't take it in – I hadn't even said goodbye to her. I should have been there, been at the hospital. I should have been sitting by her bed. I would have told her I also loved her. At least I might have had a final chance to say goodbye.

Without having been able to do any of that, everything then seemed so unreal. Her presence was still in the house. All around the room were little things of hers: a sewing basket she would never use again, an old vase she had found in an antique shop and the last item, one of her pairs of glasses. It was seeing them perched on the coffee table that was my undoing. My body just collapsed and I fell into a crying heap on the floor.

It was my grandfather who picked me up and sat me down on the settee, his hand that drew my head onto his shoulder for comfort while I sobbed and sobbed. When my crying finally ceased, he rubbed my back gently.

'Lynn, stay here, I've got to go to the boys. Your father and your grandmother will be back soon. I'll put the kettle on when I come down. Aye, this is a sad day for all of us, I know that.'

That is all I can remember of that day. The rest is just a blur and we were all numb with shock. I know my grandmother was there; she had stayed at the hospital, day and night. She would have spoken to us all. But my tears have washed it out of my mind. She was so exhausted, but insisted on driving home, which was nearby.

She promised that she would return for the funeral.

My father had sunk into a deep depression the moment the nurse had set up the little machine in their bedroom. There was no disguising the truth once that was set up by my mother's bed. He had already moved into the spare bedroom after she had her first hospital stay – 'Just so your mother can rest more,' was the reason he gave. Though I don't know how much he really slept. More than once I saw him carrying a tray up to her. Standing outside the door, he would straighten his shoulders and fix a smile onto his face before he walked in. I could hear his voice, made artificially cheery by this determination and saying, 'Here you are, darling.'

Once he came out of that room, he appeared grey and haggard, though apart from mealtimes, we hardly saw him. Over the last few weeks he had visibly aged. After her death, he gave up on putting on any sort of brave face and when he did appear, he looked unkempt and unshaven. When my grandfather spoke to him, he answered, but apart from that he ignored everyone. No matter what Grandpa cooked, he seemed to have little appetite. Not that any of us really did either. He just pushed food around his plate before getting up and going into his study. I would hear the familiar sound of a glass clinking and could picture what he was doing in there. Pouring drinks, I thought, although now he only needed one glass.

I could see that my grandfather was worried about him. Before my mother died, I overheard him once saying, 'John, you've got to put on a brave face for her and the children's sake.' To which my father replied that he could only manage to do that for his wife. Once she died though, he showed absolutely no interest in any of us. He was too wrapped up in his own misery to consider anyone else's. It was that lack of concern that made my grandfather make even more effort to look after us. Not just making sure we ate and went to bed, but trying to reassure us that our mother would not have wanted us to be so unhappy.

Like my father, Gavin seemed a ghost of his former self. He slunk in and out of rooms, hardly saying a word. I knew when he was up in his room, he was crying. Andy, who had always been a sweet-tempered and good-natured boy, began to hide his unhappiness with bursts of temper. We barely saw our father — he was still sleeping in the spare room, unable to bring himself to move back into their bedroom. Her things were still by the bed, as if she had just popped out: her watch, her glasses and the wedding ring that had become too large for her shrinking fingers. Dad ignored us and, at mealtimes, just pushed his food away and reached for the wine bottle.

My grandmother arrived a few days later to plan 'arrangements'. She too looked as though she had aged, frailer somehow. Heartbroken she must have been, but for our sakes she hid it well. Make-up was on, hair stiffly done, her clothes immaculate. It was me who opened the door to her and she enfolded me in her arms. I flung my arms around her neck, forcing back the sobs.

'You've been very brave,' she told me. 'Now, where's your father?'

'In his bedroom.'

She said nothing but I could sense her disapproval.

'So, who's looking after you?'

'Grandpa,' I told her.

'Right, and where is he, in his room too?'

'No, he's in the kitchen, cooking something for lunch.'

'What, your grandad can cook?'

'Yes,' I said, almost smiling at her surprise. 'He's pretty good too.'

'I'll talk to him there then.'

Without another word, she strode through to the kitchen, her back ramrod straight, chin up, all prepared for a confrontation that was not going to come.

'Ah, Betty love,' he said when he looked up and saw her. 'This must be a terrible time for you. You must stay for lunch. I'm doing a nice chicken casserole, plenty for everyone,' and here, he lowered his voice, 'Not that anyone's in the mood for food. Doubt if you are either, but it will do the children good to have you here.'

She only paused for a second before she said, 'Why, Joe, thank you, I will. But what I really came for was to talk to you about the children. I'm worried about them. I know Gavin's not really a child anymore but he must be taking this very hard too. Don't you think it would be best for everyone if they came and stayed with me until after the funeral at least?'

And then without waiting for a reply, she added, 'It looks like you have enough on your hands. And let's be honest, this house is no place for them at the moment. They are just children, they need to be away from everything for a while, don't you agree?'

My fingers were crossed. How I wanted her to take us to her comfy house where we would be cared for. All of us sitting on the settee together and her tucking us into a bed where the sheets smelt of lavender and the blankets were soft and fluffy. How I wanted someone who would wipe away the tears I had still not shed. I wanted to feel safe, not to have to deal with the misery that surrounded me.

'I was waiting for you to say that. You see, this is just what I think: it does not matter how old you are, grief takes its time to leave us. It's not something we can escape from. We both know that, don't we, Betty? I know losing a child is the worst thing to have to cope with. No one wants to outlive their children.'

She sighed deeply then. 'Still ...' she began.

'No,' he said before she could get any more words out. 'I know my son won't think it's a good time. He's devastated and wants his family around him.'

I saw her face stiffen, fully aware that she disliked my father. She seldom visited when she knew he would be there and never spoke of him when we visited her. Not that it was in her nature to leave the subject completely alone.

'Well, where is he? Lynn says he's in his bedroom. Sounds as though he can hardly look after himself at the moment, far less Andy and Lynn,' she said curtly. 'And these two are children, they need comfort. Then there's the funeral. Has he made any arrangements for that?'

'You mean, what's been arranged for the food and drink afterwards? That's all been taken care of. Several of Kathy's friends are doing it.'

'And the children, do you think it will be good for them to be here then?'

'Yes, Betty, I do. We've decided the little ones are not coming to the actual funeral, we think they are too young for that, but they still have to say their goodbyes. It will be good for them to see how many people loved her.'

'Well then, let me know if you need any extra help.' And by those words I knew she had capitulated. 'You have a lot on your plate, haven't you, with the running of this house. And I hear you are doing all the shopping too.'

'Gavin helps with that, he carries all the heavy stuff. And you know what? It's given me a whole new social life,' he said with something approaching a grin. 'Amazing how I can get chatting to someone in the supermarket about the price of bread and spinach!'

There was something infectious in my grandfather's smile that made her smile back at him. 'I also hear you've become a dab hand at cooking for everyone too – Lynn told me. I wanted to say something to you. In the last weeks my daughter said you were so helpful, holding the family together, I think any tension between you two was long gone.'

'That's good to hear. Yes, in the end we got along. In the kitchen it's nothing too fancy, mind, and no baking, but I'm good enough to do pot roasts.'

'Even so, it's a lot for you, Joe, plus everyone here must be grief-stricken. Everywhere you look, they must see her. I know I do.'

I saw the tears swimming in her eyes. She had now lost both her husband and her daughter and still, she was holding herself together for us.

'Sit down,' he said kindly, resting his hand on her shoulder. 'Let me make you some tea.' He poured the strong beverage into two cups. 'Maybe we should not be talking in front of Lynn. Where's Andy anyhow?' he asked me.

'In his room,' I replied.

'Well, go and get him. Tell him his grandmother's here and she wants to see him.'

I instinctively knew Grandpa had something to say that was not for my ears. He forgot though that small children are very good at eavesdropping, especially when they know they are the subject being discussed.

'Look, Betty, I'll be straight with you. I know you and my son have not always seen eye-to-eye and this would not be a good time for you to fall out, would it? That wouldn't be good for the children and they are our main concern right now. And you are right, they do need you. John's got to go back to work soon, so you just come over and see them anytime. Phone them as well.

John's not himself, as you can imagine. He's just lost his wife and he's not thinking that rationally. But you needn't worry, I'll keep an eye on everything. Of course, the children are taking it hard. Gavin's in pieces, which is why I want to keep him busy. And as for Lynn, she told me that she was happy her mother was no longer in pain. Tough little cookie, that one! But Andy now, he's really suffering. What their father believes is if they go away, they still have to come back and deal with the fact that their mother is no longer here. And school starts in just ten days. I know you want to whisk them away, but this is their home. Be reasonable, they have friends here too. I've spoken to the Headmistress, she says they will do their best to make sure that Lynn and Andy are kept an eye on, and Gavin's work is giving him time off till after the funeral. Good of them really, considering he hasn't been there that long.'

I doubt if that was the last attempt my grandmother made to have us stay with her. Knowing how much my father disliked her, I'm fairly sure he refused to budge. And he had other reasons too. I might just have confided in a woman who equally disliked him, especially in a time of mourning.

I do know that we never went to stay in her home again.

The day finally came that I had been dreading: the funeral. Andy and I really wanted to go, but all three adults told us firmly that we were too young. A sitter had been found; her name was Doris. She was a skinny, bird-like woman with a mass of curly grey hair. I liked her straight away.

'She's going to help look after you all. Not only today, but in the long term too,' my grandfather explained when we met her.

'I'm not getting any younger and it's all a bit too much for me. And your father needs to go back to work soon and you have to go to school and then there's homework to do once you are back.'

My grandmother arrived and she and Doris talked a little. Then it was time for them to go. Doris was kind; she tried to make conversation while we dully watched Gavin, my father and grandfather, all wearing black suits and black ties, leave the house. My grandmother gave us a hug and then she too was gone.

Doris did her best to try to divert us. She took us upstairs and helped select the clothes we were to wear. Not black, but navy blue for me and blue trousers and a grey blazer for Andy. Tears came when she brushed my hair and gently smoothed out its tangles.

'Mum used to do that for me,' I told her.

She did not say anything, just laid a hand on my shoulder.

Once downstairs, she made some breakfast, but when I put the food in my mouth I felt my throat close up. Andy, I saw, was feeling the same.

While we sat at that table with uneaten food in front of us, we both knew what was happening. It was my grandmother who had explained it all to us. I knew both Andy and I should have been allowed to go to the funeral, to say our goodbyes at the graveside. So, my grandmother did the next best thing and let me picture it for myself, so I could run it through my head like a film. She promised that someone would take photos of the flowers so we could see them and in time, she would take us to visit the grave once the grass had grown back over it.

They would all be in the church, prayers would be being said, a hymn sung and then the pall-bearers would pick up and carry that wooden box she was in to the freshly-dug grave. There would be another prayer, all heads would be bowed, 'Dust to dust,' the minister would intone and my father's hand would open, letting a little soil trickle onto the coffin. A few more tears would be shed and then they would all be coming back to our house to gaze at Andy and me with pity. Once I came to the end of my private film, I thought of my mother, who loved pretty things, being under that earth forever. Just thinking of it made tears start to pour down my face. All memories of her coolness to me, how when I had needed her she had pushed me away, were erased. All I could see then was her smile before her stretcher went through the door.

'I love you too, Mummy,' I said silently.

What do I remember about the people who came back to our house after the funeral? Nothing. Just a sea of faces, people bending down to talk to Andy and me, but I cannot recall a single word they said.

Chapter Fourteen

If I had loved my grandfather before my mother died, in the days that followed her funeral, I grew to love him even more. At first, I hated going back to school – I knew everyone felt sorry for me, that they did not know what to say. When children feel like that, they tend to keep away. There was one girl – her name was Michelle – who sensed both my unhappiness and my reluctance to want to talk about my mother. She took it upon herself to sit next to me in class. To begin with, I did not appreciate her friendliness, but over the next few months I grew to.

When Andy and I returned from school there was my grandfather, a smile of welcome on his face, a tea towel tucked into his belt and a plate of sandwiches and biscuits ready on the table. The kitchen would be scented with the aroma of cooking, because on the stove there was always something nourishing simmering away.

'Go and change and I'll put the kettle on for tea,' he would say each time.

Once the three of us were seated, he would ask questions about our day and what we had done at school. Homework, he decided, was easier done in the kitchen than anywhere else in the house.

'Getting a good education is important. In just a few years you will be taking those important exams, the ones that will help you get the jobs you want. So, no skipping on your homework,' was his daily mantra.

Not that he could either check our work or help us with any of our Maths or English. We knew that he had received very little schooling, so we never asked but we were aware of the effort he was making to turn an unhappy house into a home. Gradually, very gradually indeed, he seemed to be succeeding in that.

Andy's bursts of temper ceased, my father returned to work, though it seemed only part-time, and Gavin, after being allowed a couple of weeks compassionate leave, returned to the factory where we had been working since he left school.

'I've been to see the council,' Grandpa told my father over supper just a couple of weeks after my mother's death. 'You need help with this house. The children have to concentrate on their homework and I'm too old to look after everything. You've got to keep your job and start doing overseas trips again, if you need to. You can't be working part-time forever, John, now can you? Anyhow,' he continued after receiving no reply, 'Doris will come in for two days a week. The council will pay for that and if you need her to look after the children more, you will have to fork out some of your own money.'

'You two liked Doris, didn't you?'

'Yes, Dad,' we chorused.

It turned out that our father knew her; she had once worked in his company, which explained why he had not protested at her coming to work in the house.

'She's alright, is Doris,' was his only comment about her. 'And your grandpa's right, he can't do everything.'

The next morning, she arrived just before we left for school.

*

It seemed the next few weeks slipped by and the next thing we knew, it was dark nights, fires in the grate and talk about Christmas. Grandpa did his best when it was on the horizon. My father said no to a tree and any decorations and no to sending out cards full of good cheer.

'We are still in mourning,' he told my grandfather firmly.

'Yes, John, we are, so the whole family should be together. That means Kathy's as well, doesn't it?' Grandpa insisted.

'I know,' my father said irritably. 'If you want to invite Betty, it's alright, go ahead.'

Shopping lists were made, a turkey ordered, a Christmas cake baked by Betty and despite my father's objections, a few small presents bought.

All for a Christmas that would never happen.

Just a few days before Christmas Eve, my grandfather complained of an upset stomach.

'I just need an early night,' he told us.

Before he went to his room, he gave Andy and me a hug. A cold shiver went down my spine when he repeated the same words my mother had said to us when she was taken to the hospital.

'Remember, you two, I want you to always look after each other. Will you promise me that?'

We both nodded for it was something we had been doing since we were little more than toddlers anyhow. If anything, we must have looked a little puzzled.

'Oh, and your dad, he needs more looking after than you think. He misses her as well, you know, your mum.'

Another quick hug and then he went to his room.

The next morning, I was first up. I'll make Grandpa some tea and take it to him, I thought. Tell him we can get our own breakfast, if he still needs some rest.

I knocked on his door, but there was no answer. He must still be asleep, I told myself, maybe I should leave him. And then the words he had said to me the night before came flooding back, as did that icy feeling I had felt then. I could feel it spread across my body as I pushed open the door.

He was under the covers on the bed. His eyes were open, but he could no longer see me. There was a stillness, a quietness when a soul has left its body, and at the age of twelve, I felt it for the first time. After putting the tea down, I crept to the bed and sat down on the bedside chair. I gazed at the man whom I had grown to love so much.

'Oh, Grandpa,' I whispered, 'what are we going to do without you?' And then I went back to the house. His voice came into my head then, the voice that had told us so many stories about his early life.

'Us gypsies,' he once told us, 'open the window when someone departs from this world. It's so the soul can fly free.'

'I'll do that for you, Grandpa,' I said. So, I did the last thing for him that I was able to: I walked back into his room and raised the window. At least, I thought, as I left his room, I had been able to say goodbye. Then I went back to the house and woke my father.

My grandfather's funeral was the day before Christmas Eve.

If our house had been an unhappy one before, now it was a devastated one. It was such a short time since we had lost our mother. Without my grandfather, we all felt completely rudderless.

My grandmother took charge of the house over the Christmas holidays. She arranged for us to have Doris come in for two extra days. She also said that she was cooking on Christmas Day.

'There's no point letting all the food go to waste,' she told my father when he said that he had no interest in Christmas. 'I'll cook everything, the children can help. It will take their minds off things and I'll freeze whatever is left.'

She tried her best to put aside her dislike of our father for the family's sake. Even so, it was hardly a festive day – we were just pleased when it came to an end. There were no presents for there was nothing to celebrate. All we wanted was the people we had loved back.

For the next few days she busied herself filling our freezer with homemade soups and comforting meals. At the same time, she gave all three of us cookery lessons.

'You have to know the basics,' she told us. 'It means you can help out by cooking a few meals.'

She waited until after Christmas to again broach the subject of Andy and me staying with her for a while. Again, the request was flatly refused.

'We've had this conversation before, Betty,' my father said, 'and the answer is still the same: no. They have their routine, homework to do, and their school is within walking distance.'

'Well, John, if you ever want some help, or you have to go away on business, you only have to ask.'

The thanks he gave her told me, and no doubt her, that he never would.

Once my grandmother was, as my father put it, 'back in her own home, minding her own business,' he tackled another person he did not like: Gavin. It was Saturday morning and Andy and I were cooking breakfast when Dad strolled in.

'I see your grandmother taught you a few things then, Lynn,' he murmured before turning to Gavin. 'I hope she taught you something as well, because you're going to need to know how to cook where you're going.'

For a moment Gavin looked puzzled and then his expression changed to one of resignation: he knew what was coming next.

'You are old enough to fend for yourself. I want you gone today. I've found a small flat for you. I've paid the deposit and a month's rent so you can't complain I've not done my duty. Just pack up everything. I've arranged for one of my work mates to drive you there, he's coming in an hour.'

And with that he walked out of the kitchen, leaving all three of us aghast.

'Did you know about this, Lynn?' Gavin asked, 'Or you, Andy?'

'No!' we both exclaimed.

'I promise you we didn't, he never said a word,' I added.

'Why don't you go to Gran?' I asked.

'Because,' Gavin said slowly, 'if she took me in, your father would never let her in this house again. She would have to choose between you two and me. I know my mother would never have wanted this.'

I wanted to tell him I was sorry he was going. Fling my arms around him and say we would miss him. But I just couldn't. Our lives were changing so rapidly that I was frightened. What was going to happen next?

An hour later, I heard the front door open: he was gone without a goodbye. It was a very long time before I saw him again.

Chapter Fifteen

I was pleased when we went back to school – anything to get out of the house that was so full of memories. No Grandpa smiling at us when we came down for breakfast. No cooking smells perfuming the house when we returned from school. Now, it was just a cold, empty shell; any attempts at making it feel like a home had gone as my grandfather was lowered into his grave.

This time I was grateful for Michelle's overtures of friendship, which after my mother's death I had not welcomed. Then she had been new to our school: a plump little ginger-haired girl with green eyes, a freckly face and a wide, infectious smile. Her parents had only just moved into the area, she had tried to tell me, as she chatted away until I made it pretty clear I had little interest in talking to her.

She had started at our school in the term after the summer holidays. My teacher had asked me to sit next to her, no doubt thinking that looking after a new girl would take my mind off what I was going through after losing my mother. Instead, I had resented that intrusion on my grief much more than I did the reaction of those who knew both Andy and me. They, not being of an age when they had known what was the right thing to say, if anything tried to keep out of our way and, when they couldn't, just seemed awkward around us. Michelle just babbled away as though we were friends, something then I had absolutely no intention of being – I hardly wanted to talk to anyone, far less someone I didn't know. She must have had the reason for my unfriendliness explained to her, for she never appeared disconcerted by my lack of communication, just smiled at me each morning, then put her head down to her schoolwork.

The January term was different, though. I was really lonely; I even missed Gavin, especially as we had begun to put the past behind us. She was tactful enough not to mention my grandfather or anything I had gone through over the previous year. Instead, she tried to divert me with talking about anything she could that did not have any bearing on either my mother's death or my grandfather's.

Now, I actually wanted someone I could talk to during school breaks and sit with at lunchtime. I missed the lively conversations I had with my grandfather so much. In our house silence seemed never to be broken by laughter, only bursts of bad temper. I knew Andy, if anything, was even more unhappy than I was and that part of it was caused by the loss of two people we had loved, and even more so by his powerlessness to stop my father abusing me. He knew it was happening again and that he was unable to stop it.

Andy seemed to be in a world of his own. I didn't like the company he seemed to be keeping, in and out of school. They were mainly older boys, who I knew had a bad reputation.

I once asked him why he was hanging out with them.

'They're OK,' was the only answer he gave me.

So, I was grateful to have someone who greeted me with a friendly smile and kept me company.

*

A couple of weeks after the term had begun, Michelle invited me to her house for tea: Saturday afternoon, she said. I had to say that first, I must ask my father – he was not someone who would let me go out without him knowing exactly where it was to. Luckily, I caught him when he was in a rare good mood. After asking a few questions, he said, 'Alright, Lynn, as long as you do your chores first. And I expect you back before supper time. I know the food for supper only needs heating as Doris has left another casserole for us, but the vegetables and the potatoes will need peeling and that's your job.' Then, not being able to think of anything else that would restrict my time out of the house, he just added, 'I expect you and Andy to sort that out and do all the washing-up afterwards.'

I closed my ears to the additional list of chores he began to rattle off – vacuuming, bathroom cleaning, stairs sweeping – too happy that he had agreed to argue. Why so much, I wanted to scream, they are all things Doris does, except for the potatoes and the washing-up. But I knew if I challenged him, he would not agree to me going out to tea. Resolving to get up early and make sure they were done, I thought I would ask Andy to help me anyhow.

How very much the two of us missed our grandfather on those dull winter days. Grey skies and grey shadows and coming back from school to an empty house. No wrinkled, smiling face to greet us, no food simmering in the kitchen. When we changed out of our school clothes, there was no cup of tea or a plate of biscuits waiting. How we hated coming home from school on the days when Doris was not there. She was always so chatty and not only that, she brought homemade cakes for us.

Although we had central heating, Dad always insisted the large lounge fire was lit every night. It was our job to clean out the last night's ashes, carry in wood and coal, lay and then light the fire before washing up the breakfast dishes that were piled in the sink. If Doris was not in that day, we would sort out from the fridge which meal we were eating. I would peel potatoes and chop up some vegetables. Then Andy and I would make ourselves a sandwich and tea and, putting on the TV, sit in front of a now-crackling fire, plates on our knees – something that was strictly not permitted when our father was home. Quiet as the house was, it was a lot more peaceful without his morose presence.

My father's depression, which had started before our mother died, had become far worse since his father followed his wife to the grave so soon afterwards. It seemed to have taken over his life, as though a thick black cloud had settled on his shoulders and one that he had no intention of shrugging off, not for his own sake and certainly not for ours. His depression did not stop him abusing me, though, for it did not take him long after the second funeral to begin again.

It started on a night when he poured not one drink but two from the bottle labelled whisky.

'One for you too, Lynn, you're nearly a teenager and teenagers are allowed a drink, aren't they?' he reasoned, handing it to me and clinking his glass against mine. 'Swallow it now, you'll soon grow to like it.'

This was not, I knew, a treat suitable for a child. One look in his eyes told me that. There was no smile lurking in their depths, no warmth at all. Instead, a blankness that chilled me.

It was as though he was not seeing me at all, or even worse, it was someone else he imagined standing there in front of him. I knew better than to argue and obediently swallowed it down quickly. It was not a taste I liked – in fact, I almost gagged. I could not understand why grown-ups made such a fuss about drinking alcohol.

That Saturday family tea at Michelle's opened my eyes to what a normal family was like around each other. Even in my early memories of childhood when guests came to tea we wore new clothes for the time that they were there. Any form of entertaining felt staged, not just a normal family occasion.

Here, homemade scones were on the table, there was lively conversation and little jokes were bantered between her parents.

'He wants to watch a football match on TV,' Michelle explained with a giggle when her dad told us he should get out of our way. 'You three can have a girls' chat,' were his actual words.

The afternoon passed so quickly, before I knew it, I had to leave to get home by the appointed time.

'You could stay here for supper,' Michelle said with a look of optimism. And how I wanted to, but knowing how much trouble that would cause at home, I just thanked them for the offer and used the excuse that my father would be preparing the evening meal. But the next time I told him I had been invited for tea again, he said no and I soon found his agreeing to my visit had been a one-off and any more requests were met with resistance: 'You've got homework to do' or 'There's work to do in the house'. In other words, any excuse he could think of to stop me going.

'I've thought of a plan that will get Dad to let you visit your friend more often,' Andy told me one day with an unexpected wide smile.

'What?' I said without much hope that whatever he was going to suggest would work.

'Remember we got the better of him once over us bathing together and why? He's worried about what people think of him, true?'

'Yes,' I said, my interest suddenly perking up.

'I'll tell you what,' explained Andy, 'you go and visit her after school and I'll sort the supper out that he makes so much fuss about. After a few times confide in her that Dad is being over-protective, say you know he's depressed and scared of letting you out of his sight. Now, I'm sure her mother will understand that. I think after a few visits you can begin to drop a few hints that maybe if he met her, he would feel reassured that you would be looked after alright. So, while I'm peeling those vegetables that he keeps going on about and getting the fire lit, you can be having a nice time with your friend. Now, what do you think of my plan, Lynn?'

'I think it might just work. Oh thanks, Andy, you're a star!' I said with a grin, feeling like hugging him.

'One day, we'll get away from him,' he said then. 'But in the meantime ...'

'... well, we have to win a few little battles,' we said in unison, quoting one of our grandfather's favourite sayings.

My brother gave me a hug, saying, 'This will get sorted, you just wait.'

I liked Andy's plan. It could really work, I thought, with the beginning of a smile. And over the course of a couple of weeks,

I put it into action. I made little remarks at the tea table, 'Oh, is that the time? I must get a move on. Dad will be home soon and he'll be worried if I'm not there.'

'Won't Andy tell him you're with me and we're doing our homework together?' asked Michelle.

'Yes, but he still gets worried about me walking home in the dark.'

That was the beginning of me dropping little bits of information that I knew Michelle would repeat to her mother. Which she had clearly and I knew for sure when her mother Maggie mentioned it to me.

'I can understand why your dad doesn't want his children let out of his sight,' she said sympathetically. 'After all, you are all he's got now so it's not surprising really that he's being a bit over-protective. Still, it's good for you to have friends, so we will have to show him that. I'm sure he has only your best interests at heart. I think it would be a good idea if I popped round to see him, reassure him that we will always get you home safely.'

I stopped the grin going over my face and just agreed that I thought that would work. Of course, she believed that he was just an over-protective father, not one who did not want me to make friends. His concern was not my safety but that I might just pluck up courage to confide in someone.

Again, I had the chance to tell her a little of the truth, but again, I was unable to speak out. The memory of that night when he had threatened us with the orphanage had never left my mind. Partly the fear of also losing Andy stilled my tongue, as did the fear of her no longer wanting me in her house.

I gave her the time we had supper and she told me she would turn up just after. I did mention that it might be better if my father didn't know I was expecting her – I didn't want him thinking I had asked her.

'Be best if my dad believes it's all your idea,' I said without thinking that I should also have asked her not to mention just how often I was actually at her house. So, just two weeks after Andy hatched his little plot, our doorbell rang one evening when we were clearing up after supper.

It was my father who answered the door and seeing a woman my mother's age, assumed she must have been an old friend of his wife's. One he might possibly have met, but not remembered. I could hear her saying she was Michelle's mother and him inviting her in. I know his smile appeared, the charming one, because it was still fixed on his face when they came into the kitchen.

'Lynn, your friend's mother has just come to see us. Put the kettle on, would you, pet?'

Pet! I thought, almost laughing out loud. He's really putting on the devoted father act.

'I'll bring the tea into the lounge,' I told him with a smile as I placed some biscuits on a plate. If he could act his role, then so could I.

'I thought I'd better come and introduce myself to you, Mr Murray,' she was explaining as I walked in with the tray. 'We do so enjoy your daughter's visits after school.'

'Oh, call me John, please,' I heard him say and out came that charming smile again. One that did not give away that she had just told him something he had not known.

'It's just as my daughter and yours have become such good friends, I would like to invite Lynn over for a day. We could all do something together. I thought I might take both girls to the cinema.'

My father was not a man who wanted to appear to be unreasonable, which left him with little choice but to agree.

'What a lovely idea, Maggie, very kind of you. It would be good for Lynn,' he told her before he managed to inject his subtle reason why it should not happen too often. 'I suppose I have been a bit selfish, wanting her with me at weekends. It's just that's the only time I really get to see her, apart from us having a quick meal together. Demands of my job, you know. I had so much time off when my wife was ill.'

Then, leaning forward slightly, he went on to tell her another reason why I was needed at home: 'It's just that she's very close to her brother. He's taken what's happened over the last few months very badly. Another reason I always try and do family things at the weekend.'

The first I'd heard of it, I thought sourly, stopping my jaw from gaping open.

'It's the only really free time I have to spend with them, I used all my leave up for the year when my father died,' he added for good measure. 'But I'm sure we can work something out, Maggie. Got to give them more freedom really, I know that. And now I've met you, I know Lynn will be in safe hands,' he said, throwing me a Devoted Dad smile.

'Well, how about her having supper with us next Friday?' asked Maggie. 'I'll bring her home afterwards.'

My father agreed with this suggestion with an apparent willingness, though, as I had expected, he took his bad temper out on me later. He waited until her car had disappeared before calling Andy down and then let his temper boil over as he shouted at us. Accusations like 'liars', 'not to be trusted' and we 'had let him down' flew around us until finally, he told us to get out of his sight. Something we were both happy to do. Contrary to expectation, he did not hit me that night.

As Andy and I headed upstairs to our rooms, he seemed confident his plan had worked: 'We got off lightly there,' he murmured, although I guessed Dad had something up his sleeve and I was right.

Even so, the friendship of Michelle and her family helped heal the gaping emptiness in my life.

Chapter Sixteen

A few evenings after Michelle's mother had paid us a call, it became clear what type of revenge my father had planned for Andy and me.

It was one of those evenings when he had managed to lull us into a false sense of security. We had been waiting for some punishment to be handed out, but nothing more had been said. We had almost begun to think that he had forgotten about that visit. On the Wednesday, even though our fridge had been restocked by Doris, he told us not to bother with the supper: he was going to bring home pizzas, which he knew we loved. Time we had a bit of a treat, he said, and he would pick them up on the way home.

Which he did, plus he even remembered to bring two cola drinks for Andy and me, although I did notice there was also a bottle of wine on the table for him. Over the first part of the evening he seemed to be in an unusually good mood. He asked questions about what we had done over the day, how school had been, and then brought up the subject of GCEs. Had Andy given any thought to what would be his most important subjects?

'You, at thirteen, might see three years as being a long way ahead,' he said with a pleasant smile. 'But wait till you reach my age. Then you will realise just how fast the years fly by. Why, it only seems like yesterday since you pair were born. So, Andy, you being the eldest, must start thinking of your future. Homework is really important now, as is consistently good grades. It's vital you concentrate on that so I want you both to come straight home from school and get those schoolbooks out. No popping in to see friends on the way back, you can do that in the holidays.'

Before we could get a word in, such as all our homework was always done and most of it had been given at least B grades and often A's, he continued, hardly pausing for breath.

'Now, a little bit of good news for you, Andy. I'm letting you have the room over the garage, you will have all the peace and quiet you need up there to study. There are still some things of your grandfather's there, so you can give me a hand over the weekend, packing it up. I'll get some coffee and tea, milk and a few bits and pieces for the fridge so you can make your own hot drinks and with the shower up there, you won't even have to share a bathroom with your sister and me any longer.'

Then turning to me, with that pleasant smile still fixed on his face, he added, 'You can give us a hand too, Lynn. Needs a good clean-out and I don't think that's Doris's job, is it?' Again, he beamed as though delighted at the surprise he had just given us. Of course, he was delighted, but not for the reasons he was trying to portray.

'Now, aren't you going to say thank you, Andy? Not many boys of your age would actually have their own separate flat.'

'Thanks, Dad,' my brother managed to choke out. Maybe he thought just for a few moments that our father was being sincere, a belief that was dashed very quickly.

'Oh, by the way, more good news,' Dad added, 'I've had my hours cut down a little at work, means I'll be back at the same time as you from school on some days. Pity is, I never know which ones they will be.'

At this we felt the same as how I imagine two small flies must feel after flying straight into a spider's web: totally helpless. We both knew his reasons for hatching that little plan. There would be no more slipping into each other's rooms at night for a chat. As soon as supper was over, Andy would be expected to disappear. Nor could we risk spending much time together in the afternoons – our father would expect Andy to be working away above the garage as soon as we reached home. And I realised that I would not be free to pop round to Michelle's house on the way back from school. In one move he had managed to make our lives even more isolated and him in even more control of them.

Something his next remark made even clearer: 'I know this arrangement will mean you having more work to do, Lynn. Apart from bringing in coal and logs, I don't want Andy doing housework. Still, there's Doris – she does most of it, doesn't she? Pity I can't get her more than once a week, but that's this government for you and I can't afford to pay her out of my own pocket, especially as I'm now on reduced hours at work.'

We stared at the now-empty wine bottle, silently coming to the same conclusion: the cost of the wine and whisky he brought home each week would come to more than a day's wages for Doris.

'Still,' he said in that reasonable tone of voice that made me want to scream, 'I know you want what's best for your brother, Lynn, so I'm sure you won't mind, will you?'

What could I say but, 'No, Dad, of course not'?

We both knew that it was the beginning of our father getting more ways to control us; to know exactly where we were every minute. Not only that, once Andy was in Grandpa's old room, there would be just my father and me sleeping in the house. He would be free to do whatever he liked with me without Andy knowing more than I told him.

'We should tell someone. This is so he can abuse you without me hearing,' Andy told me fiercely once we were upstairs. 'I know what he does to you and I know it's really wrong.'

'Tell who, Andy?' I said miserably. 'Who'd believe us? They would ask why we hadn't mentioned it before, not even to our grandmother. Dad would say that I had made up stories before to cause trouble. He'd say I'm doing it again because we are not getting our way in everything and all you know is what I've told you or overheard. And don't you remember what he said when you told our mother that he had touched you as well as me? That he would put us in a home, only separate ones. We'd never see each other. And you know he would do it – look how quick he was to get rid of Gavin.'

'I almost think he's the lucky one, not us,' said Andy. 'He's out of this place, isn't he? I just can't wait till we're old enough to leave.'

Both of us just looked at each other, defeat written all over our faces. Andy hugged me, but there was nothing left to say. Neither of us slept well that night. At that age we had no idea that I would have been believed, that there was help and that we could have escaped.

Chapter Seventeen

My memories of the two years between my twelfth birthday and my fourteenth one are an array of jumbled-up incidents. Certainly, the months between that August and Christmas are. The ones after that period are a little less blurry to recall accurately. Most of them are intensely unhappy ones, where pain and humiliation played a great part. Were there any nice times? There must have been, otherwise I would never have survived my childhood. One good thing in my life then was my friendship with Michelle and the other was the bond between Andy and me.

And my father, how did I feel about him? I think that for most of my childhood my feelings towards him were actually quite mixed. I still believed then that in his own way he loved us. I don't know why I believed it, but I did. Perhaps that is what actually kept me sane. And just for that reason alone, I allowed myself to make excuse after excuse for his behaviour. It was those excuses that made me push aside the severity of many of his actions and almost feel pity for him, a feeling I know Andy did not share with me.

Whereas my father, who had been a moderate drinker when my mother was alive, had within a few months of his father's death turned into a heavy one. Not that I objected to that, for when he was passed out in a drunken stupor, sat in front of the TV long into the early hours, I knew he would not visit my bedroom that night.

The bad times that sent fear coursing through my body were when he was drunk enough to turn nasty and aggressive. It would start with sarcastic words designed to hurt. Each time I would hope that he would just pour yet another drink and pass out. When he didn't, those were the times my father forgot to be careful with my body and an assortment of bruises often appeared. Some came from slaps, others were caused by strong, bony fingers pressing hard into my soft flesh.

Whichever cruelty had caused them, they made me feel branded. I felt I would be shunned if anyone guessed what had caused them. And that fear made me skilled at making up excuses. 'I slipped, Miss', 'I knocked myself, Michelle' were just some of the excuses that I was forced to use. At school, when it was time for PE classes, I often pretended to have a cold or simply said I was not feeling well. No one was going to be too hard on a girl who had lost both her mother and her grandfather in the same year. Not that I must have looked well when, with face burning, I stuttered out my various excuses. I could not bear the thought of those telltale marks and scratches being exposed for everyone to see.

The gym teacher looked a little worried when I used that excuse once too often. Usually a hand would touch my forehead, followed by her saying, 'Mmm, you do feel a little hot, maybe best if you don't join in today.' And so I was let off and free to go to the school library and do my homework. But the last time I made that excuse, she took me to her office and sat me down.

'Lynn, do you know what periods are?'

'Yes, Miss – Doris explained it all to me.'

'I just wondered if you had started. That might be the reason you looked a little flushed and you did tell me you had a bit of stomach cramp.'

'No,' I told her, blushing with embarrassment, 'not yet.'

There must have been something about me that day that concerned her, for later on I was called into the Head's office. She asked questions about how I was coping with my bereavements, which of course I expected. I just said that my father was in most evenings and that Doris sorted out most of the cooking and cleaning. She also asked what tasks Andy and I were given.

I suppose I must have played it down a little, but she did not appear totally happy with my answers. She was still concerned about us, I knew.

'My door is always open, Lynn. If you ever feel you need to talk, you will come to me?'

'Thank you, Miss, I will,' was all I could muster.

And yet another chance of being saved from my abusive home life disappeared, without me even knowing it had been there.

My grandmother tried to visit us as much as possible and my father, in his turn, tried to put her off with as many excuses as he could muster. Homework being one, my visits to Michelle another, and I'm fairly convinced he probably conjured up a few more. But he must have been careful of going too far, for he would not have wanted her to become suspicious. His compromise was to invite her over for the occasional Sunday lunch. This was the one meal that he was still prepared to cook himself, with just a little bit of help from Andy and me. It was calculated to make us appear to her as a functioning family, working together to get through our grief. I knew frequent invitations came from her as well, but he never gave in on the issue of us staying with her.

He must have been constantly on his guard about us getting too friendly with any adult that we might find the confidence to talk to about the reality of our home life. And wouldn't our grandmother have been the most obvious choice? No wonder he tried to avoid too much contact and was always present when she was there, just in case we aroused her suspicions.

One day I overheard her voicing her opinion on Gavin leaving: 'He's lost two people as well, John. Don't you think he should have stayed here a bit longer?'

'He wanted his independence,' my father stated adamantly, 'and I helped out, didn't I? I put down his deposit and paid the first month's rent on his flat, so he's got nothing to grumble about.'

'And when did you all see him last?'

There was a silence that lasted a little too long at that question. For the truth was that my father hadn't once mentioned Gavin to us after he had left, far less bothered to see if he was alright. And Gavin had never tried to make contact; I doubt if he thought he would have been welcome if he had. I could sense the tension hanging in the air, which my grandmother decided to break.

'Well, he's doing alright,' she said, 'he seems settled in his flat and has started to enjoy that job in the furniture factory. He's hoping they will in time let him do some designing too. He was my first grandchild, John, so naturally, I worry a little about him.'

Then, with a certain degree of tactfulness, she managed to change the subject. It seemed as if my father had forgotten that Gavin was her grandchild as well. Nothing more was said on the subject but I knew that my grandmother did not believe a word of what he had said about it having been Gavin's choice. On the other hand, if she didn't let it go, she ran the risk of falling out with my father completely. If that happened, her chances of seeing Andy and me would be even more jeopardised.

Over the few months since Andy had been 'given', as my father put it, the small studio apartment above the garage, he came down even heavier on me about housework. There were times when I was brave enough to ignore the frown settling on his face as I tried to stand up for myself.

'Why don't you let it wait until Doris is here?' I asked him more than once when he told me to do something that she had done just a couple of days earlier. 'I mean, there's only the two of us here most of the time and we're hardly making it dirty, are we?'

'Well then, I'd better put you in charge of something she does not have time to do; all your and Andy's washing and mine too, of course. You'll need to strip the beds and remake them too. That can be your Sunday chore. There's too much for just one wash, isn't there? Oh, and Lynn,' my father added after I had managed to take note of my new weekend routine, 'there will be a lot of ironing for Doris, so you can vacuum the lounge and the stairs and don't forget to clean the bathroom either.'

'Clean the bathroom,' I muttered under my breath, for it was not me who left damp towels on the floor and a tidemark of soapy scum in the bath. Nor did I leave shaving foam with tiny bits of hair in it stuck to the sides of the washbasin either.

So, on Sunday mornings, I stripped my bed and my father's too and gathered up towels, sorted out my school shirts and gym clothes, as well as emptying the laundry basket stuffed with Dad's washing. Andy brought his own into the kitchen. He tried to hang around to help, but was either given something else to do like shopping in town, or whatever else my father could think of, that got him away from me.

There are a few vivid memories that have stuck in my mind from that time, ones that I can still see very clearly today. It happened on a weekend. I remember that it was a Sunday because that was the day I had to take care of all our washing; Saturday was the one where I cleaned. It is embedded in my mind. How I did laundry then was not how I do it now: open the machine door, throw everything in, then sit down with a cup of coffee while it whirls away. No, when I was twelve, we still had the old-fashioned twin tub – one that had to be filled by fixing a hose onto the cold tap and then waiting for the water to heat. In our house, washing was a task that took almost the whole day. The machine was old, for my parents had had it a long time – since they got married, I think – and my father insisted as it was built to last, that was what it must do. He had always given my mother the latest things but on this matter he was steadfast. Mind you, back then a new automatic washing machine was a big purchase, far more so than it is today.

It was an onerous task that I absolutely hated, for it was hot, steamy work. Noisy as well, as once I got it going, it thumped and thundered the dirt out of our clothes. Once that cycle was finished came the part I disliked more than anything: pulling very hot, dripping-wet clothes out of the top of the machine and putting them in the second tub, which was for rinsing. When that drained, there was a short spin, but the clothes were still pretty sodden when they were hung out to dry. Wet clothes, I found out, were twice as heavy as dry ones. Every Sunday, as I woke up, I used to think miserably that this was not how I wanted to spend my day. At school, all my peers were telling stories about their weekends and what they had done, conversations I could hardly join in.

That particular morning started off like all my Sundays: sorting out the washing. I had asked my father whether, once I had all the washing on the line, I could visit Michelle. My request was greeted with no explanation, just the word no.

'Anyhow,' he added ten minutes or so later, as he climbed the stairs back up to his bedroom, 'there are at least two loads today, so you won't be finished early.'

I was just thinking how miserable I felt and how unfair my life was when there was a knock on the door. Opening it, I was greeted by my smiling friend, who said she had come round to cheer me up.

'I knew you probably couldn't come to mine,' Michelle said as we walked into the kitchen, surveying the mountain of clothes, 'so I thought I'd come to you. So, where's your dad?'

'He's upstairs, taking a nap,' I told her, although sleeping off another hangover would have been closer to the truth.

'When did you put the water in?' she asked, and as soon as I told her it had only just gone in, she said, 'Oh, it will take ages to heat up. I know our old machine always did,' for her mother had recently acquired a new front-loading Bosch. 'Let's go down to the shop and get some lemonade and a bag of fruit gums, what do you say?'

'I can't,' I said nervously, 'my dad ...' And with that my voice trailed off and I found myself glancing up at the stairs, 'my dad will be cross if he wakes up and I'm not here, and anyhow, I haven't any money.'

'Well, I have,' was her prompt response. 'Come on, Lynn, I'll treat you and we'll be back in a few minutes, won't we?'

If there were twelve- or thirteen-year-olds who could resist the temptation of sweets and a fizzy drink, I wasn't one of them. The sun was shining, Michelle was grinning and I wanted just a little time out to feel free. Thinking my father was unlikely to wake, I just asked myself why not, and ran down the road to the corner shop with her. But my luck was not in that day. Even though I doubt if we were gone for longer than ten minutes, it was long enough for my father to have woken up and come down into the kitchen.

Excessive alcohol, I have learnt as an adult, stays in the system for twenty-four hours, affecting both judgement and self-control. Well, that was certainly true of how my father acted that day. There was no sign of his charming public face that he was always so careful to show to visitors, when his eyes rested angrily on Michelle. Instead, it was almost purple with rage and the anger he unleashed was not just directed in my direction, but to both of us.

'You might not have to help your mother,' he shouted at Michelle as his eye caught sight of the bottles and packets we were holding, 'but seeing my daughter hasn't got one, she has to help me. She's got her chores to do and she's not got time to see friends whose only interest is spending their pocket money on fizzy drinks and sweets! Her days aren't spent playing pointless games either.'

Michelle looked completely shocked for I am sure she had never seen anyone spoken to like that, far less herself. But she was not a girl lacking in courage: she squared her shoulders and glared back at Dad.

'Surely she's allowed a tiny tea break, Mr Murray? Even our cleaner has one – Mum says it's the law. So, I thought you wouldn't mind Lynn taking a small one as well.'

At least my father restrained himself from lashing out at her physically.

'Get out of my house,' he shouted, 'and don't come back!'

'Lynn, are you going to be alright? I can ask my mother to come round if there's a problem,' she said.

'No, thanks, Michelle,' I said quietly, knowing it would only make the situation worse.

Andy appeared as if from nowhere. 'Dad,' he said assertively, 'you know who she is, her mother's Maggie, the lady who visited us. She's not a stranger who has crept in here, she's a good friend of Lynn and mine from school.'

The expression on our father's face changed then. A quick apology was muttered but his eyes remained averted. He said he was sorry and he explained that he had not been well. I could tell that Michelle did not believe this apology or the half-proffered excuse for one moment. She said a quick goodbye, touching my hand in support.

'See you at school, Lynn. Chin up,' she whispered as she left.

'I'll help Lynn with the washing,' Andy told our father firmly. 'Let's hope Michelle says nothing to her mother.'

Andy told me later why he had spoken up: 'I wasn't trying to stop him for his sake,' he said, 'but for yours. Michelle's mother would definitely have stopped her ever coming round here again if it had got any worse. I think he was only a step away from hitting her. Her mum could have told the Headmistress what happened here.'

I think his verbal attack on Michelle frightened my father. He stayed in bed for the rest of that day. For once he had actually taken the clean and ironed bedding that Doris had left and made up his own and my bed; Andy's bedding was waiting on a chair on the landing. Was he ashamed of his behaviour, I wondered.

But if Andy and I thought we had won, we were very wrong. That was just the beginning of our father's rapid descent, one that was going to take us all down with it.

Chapter Eighteen

When my mother was alive it was she who brushed my hair and trimmed it regularly. After her death, my grandfather had continued with it: 'A little bit of barbering,' he called it when, with scissors, brush and comb at the ready, he sat me down in the kitchen. He often compared it to brushing the pony's tail and mane when he was growing up – 'We gypsies were very proud of our ponies, Lynn, so they always got groomed by us laddies.' Since his death it had been left and had grown way beyond my shoulders. Each night and morning, I tried to brush it, even though after a couple of months, my brush stopped going through so easily. Not only that, gradually each brushstroke on the back of my head began to be very painful.

I used a mirror to see the back and there were these tangles, all knotted together like a bird's nest. I thought they made my hair look unwashed and made sure each morning that the sides were pinned back so they were hidden. I was too embarrassed by them to ask for help – I didn't want Michelle's mother to think of me as dirty or have a teacher remark on it. In the end, when the back of my head even hurt as I lay on my back in bed, I went to Doris.

'Could you help me, Doris?' I asked. I know I looked tearful for my head had hurt even more that morning and I had hardly been able to put a brush through my hair – I'd just tied it all back and gone to school. By the time I reached home, it was aching.

'Of course, love. What's the problem?' Then, glancing at me, she stretched out her arm and drew me closer to her: 'Come here, Lynn. You know can tell me anything, that's one of the reasons I'm here, you know.'

It felt so good to feel her warmth as she hugged me to her. At that point I almost burst into tears. I felt tired and my body still ached from my father coming into my room the night before. And now my head hurt as well. Not only that, I was getting even more frightened by my father's unpredictable temper. That scene he made when he saw Michelle had unnerved me. If Andy had not heard it and known the right words to say, I dread to think what might have happened. Michelle had tried to reassure me that it was just between us; she said it was better if her mother did not hear about it. But still, I fretted that her mother would find out and stop us being friends.

I know it's a pretty big understatement to say that my father had never been an easy man to live with. For years, I had never known if he was going to hit me, abuse me or just throw out insults. But there had always been flashes of good nature and he had never been rude to a guest before. This was something new, which made me feel that the man I was under the same roof as had become a stranger to me. Not that I told Doris any of that, I just told her my head hurt when I tried to brush my hair.

'Good God, child!' she exclaimed when she picked up a section of hair and saw what was underneath. 'Of course, it's hurting you, it's matted right down to your scalp. I'm going to have to cut those knots out.'

'Mum used to brush them out,' I whispered, suddenly remembering the feel of her body as I leant against her when she ran the brush through my hair. More tears threatened to choke me when I thought of the last few times she had managed to do it for me. She was getting weaker and holding the brush was becoming too difficult for her. My life might have not been happy while she was alive, but it was a lot worse now. And I missed her.

Seeing that just mentioning my mother had brought on my tears again, Doris put her arms round my shoulders tightly and cuddled me for a few moments.

'Come on, Lynn, we'll get this sorted and then your head won't hurt. I can't believe you've been tying back the sides to hide it. Oh love, why didn't you say something? It's nothing to be ashamed of, it must have been hurting you for quite a while. And what do you think I'm here for, eh? One of the main reasons your grandmother organised it was so I can keep an eye on you and Andy.'

'I should have been able to do it myself,' I said, 'I'm not a little girl anymore, am I? I'm twelve – well, nearly thirteen, actually. Other girls manage, don't they?'

'Other girls don't have hair like yours, Lynn. It's lovely, your thick curly hair, but it's not so easy to look after. Now, I'll tell you what we're going to do,' she said, sitting me up and dabbing my tears away, 'we're going to go upstairs and wash it and put lots of conditioner on it. I'll leave it in while I work on those nasty knots, then a quick rinse and I'll give your hair a good trim. I think really short will suit you, very fashionable teenager look. Alright?'

'Yes,' I said gratefully, excited at the idea of a grown-up style.

'And after I've trimmed it, I'll show you how to look after it yourself. Alright, love?'

'Now,' she asked a little later when I was sat on a kitchen chair and she was trimming away at my hair, 'there's a lot of washing been done. Who does all that, your father?'

'No, it's me. It's one of my jobs.'

'And what other jobs do you have?'

'Just cleaning,' I told her and explained that although my father wanted Andy to concentrate on his homework, my brother still gave me a hand whenever he could. I did not mention that had to be when Dad was not about.

'Well, what I can't really understand is why he wants all the sheets washed and changed before I come. I'm quite capable of doing them, I'm here twice a week. I'll have a word with him.'

I wanted to say 'Don't, it will get me into trouble' but I knew that would only make things worse.

Later, I heard Doris talking to my father. I don't know what it was that he had said to her – most probably, I was old enough to help out and anyhow, daughters were meant to pull their weight in the house – because that's what he said to me on more than one occasion. Whatever it was, he certainly provoked her. There was no mistaking the anger in her voice.

'She's a child, Mr Morris! And I'd almost say she's being neglected. If I see her in that state again, I'm off to social services. Remember, it's them who pay me, not you, and they pay me to keep an eye on the children as well as keeping your house clean. I don't expect to hear that she's been doing my work again. There's no reason for that and she too has homework to do, as well as her brother. Now I can make some allowances, what with you grieving, but still, it's not a good enough excuse. You understand?'

'Yes, I'll sort it out,' he said in a conciliatory tone, one that did not fool me in the least. There was a reason he did not want Doris to change my bed: she might see the evidence of what was going on in my bedroom at night. But what I didn't know was how he would react once she had gone.

No sooner had she left than he called me into the lounge.

'Sit down, Lynn, we're going to have a little chat. Now, answer me truthfully, did you tell Doris that you did all the cleaning?'

'I told her I did some.'

'And what about the washing?'

'Well, yes, she did ask. She had noticed that it was done and our beds were stripped and remade.'

'Alright, I want you to tell me exactly what you said to her. What were you talking to her about?'

'She was sorting out the mess my hair was in and she asked about the washing – she wanted to know who did it. She said she could change the beds and put the washing on, that's all.'

His tone of voice changed to a conciliatory one but that did not fool me one bit.

'Now, did you say anything else to her?' he said, his eyes meeting mine with what I can only describe as a searching look.

'Just that Mum used to sort my hair out, then Grandpa did it for me. That's why Doris had to cut it so short, she had to get rid of all the knots. She said curly hair as thick as mine is not easy to manage.'

'Well, you could have come to me, couldn't you? Anyhow, it looks nice short, it's very feminine,' he said with one of his pleasant smiles. 'So, that's all you two talked about?'

'Honestly, Dad, that was all.'

'Good, because we have had this discussion before, haven't we? What would happen if either you or Andy tried to cause any trouble for our family? And it's not something I want to repeat.'

'Yes, we have,' I said, though I did not point out that we hardly had a family any longer.

As if reading my mind, my father said, 'Oh, we might be a smaller family now than we were a year ago, but you still have Andy, don't you?'

'Yes.'

'And you wouldn't want him to disappear from your life, would you?'

'No,' I said and those treacherous tears began to well up again.

'There's no need to cry, Lynn. You sort out your homework and I'll make supper, that alright for you?'

'Yes, Dad.'

My father's relief that he had convinced Doris that everything was alright in our home must have disappeared when he received a call from social services not long after that talk with her. Not that they mentioned Doris, or that she had spoken to them about her concerns, it was just a routine call was what they told him. They explained that, as Andy and I were still quite young, they were assigning us a family social worker, who would visit once a week.

Not that my father mentioned that call to us until the day the social worker was due to arrive. A 'routine visit' was how he explained it to us. 'One,' he added, 'to see how we are coping as a family.' Her name was Julia was all he knew about her and she would be arriving a little after we got home from school.

'You needn't worry that you will have to see her on your own,' he told us in his new friendly voice. 'I'll leave work early, I'll probably be back before you are.'

'Means he doesn't want us talking to anyone from social services on our own is what I think,' Andy said as we walked to school.

'That explains why he's been off the drink and being quite nice,' I deduced. 'I have been wondering why that was.'

'I did too. So now we know. Anyhow, I'm sure we won't be left alone with her for a second, you see if I'm right.'

He was.

When we arrived back on the day of the visit it was to be greeted by the nice father we hadn't seen for so long. Sandwiches had been made, the kettle was boiling, all the breakfast things had been washed up and put away, and he had also done a fair amount of grocery shopping. There were vegetables sitting in the rack near the fridge and on the table was a bowl I had not seen for months, filled with an assortment of fruit.

The perfect family was back, or what was left of it.

It was my father who answered the door to her. I heard him saying, 'Let's talk in the kitchen, it's where Lynn does her homework.'

And where she will be able to see that he has our tea ready, I thought.

There was nothing intimidating about the young woman who came into the kitchen. Somewhere in her late twenties, wearing a denim skirt and a light blue cotton jumper, her dark blonde hair tied back in a ponytail. A warm smile was directed at Andy and me. She looked more like a young mum than a career woman was the thought that ran through my head.

My father did not seem to see her as a threat either. Tea was offered, a charming smile given and small talk made. I saw her give me an appraising look, not that she said much to either Andy or me that first time.

'It's nice to meet you all together,' she said, before telling Andy and me to call her Julia, not 'Miss'. 'I will be dropping in once a week, just to see how you are all coping. I know you have all been through a lot and sometimes it's good to know there's another pair of ears to listen and have someone outside the family who you can talk to.'

She then asked us to take our tea into the lounge so that she could talk to our father in private, 'I just need to make a few notes on the children's routines,' was all we heard and as we left the room, she got out a large notebook from her briefcase.

'Checking to see if they match up with what she's heard from Doris, I bet,' Andy whispered to me once we were out of earshot in the lounge.

I was sure my father made certain they did.

Julia left fairly soon after that, put her head round the lounge door to say goodbye and told us she would be seeing us soon. I heard my father telling her it was a pleasure to have met her and then the door closed.

Chapter Nineteen

A few days later, Doris asked me what I had thought of Julia. I could tell she was disappointed when I explained that I had hardly spoken to her.

'Well, Dad was there the whole time,' I pointed out, 'but she seemed nice enough. She and Dad sent Andy and me into the sitting room so they could have a chat about "our routine", whatever that means.'

What I did not tell Doris about was the drive my father had taken Andy and me on afterwards.

On the Saturday after Julia's visit, he suggested we clear out all our old toys and clothes that no longer fitted us. Mum always did that but what with her illness, it had been neglected. We had outgrown many clothes and really didn't play with toys anymore.

'Bring them into the hall when you have finished,' he told us. 'It will give you both more cupboard space, won't it?'

We were a little puzzled by his request for this kind of sorting out was not something he had shown much interest in before. After our mother's death it was our grandfather who had packed up everything that belonged to her. He had given me a few things but her jewellery, he assured me, would be kept safe until I was older. Not wanting any of us to see her familiar clothes in a charity shop window, he had been thoughtful enough to take them to a neighbouring town.

My father's voice broke into my reverie: 'Bring it all down when you have it sorted,' I heard him saying. 'And I expect to see a decent-sized pile so no hoarding things you no longer have any use for. I shall be inspecting your rooms to make sure of that.'

True to his word, once we had brought everything down, he went first into my room with me following behind him.

'What, you're still keeping your dolls at your age, Lynn? No, they're going,' he said, gathering my favourite ones up. I know I was almost a teenager, but the dolls helped remind me of happier times. Even the blonde-haired one he had brought me back from one of his early trips to Germany was tucked under his arm, before being dumped in the hall callously. I bit my lip to stop myself from crying when I saw it there.

Next, it was Andy's turn: 'Now, if I go to your old room and the flat, am I going to find anything that should be thrown out?' my father asked him. Before my brother had a chance to say no, he was told to go back and take another look: 'And if you come back empty-handed, I shall have to go and look for myself and I'm sure you don't want to make me do that, do you? So, back you go, son.'

It took us all morning. There were things both Andy and I hated parting with, but we understood there was no point in protesting. Once Dad was satisfied there was very little left in our rooms that we wanted to keep, he pushed everything into four bin liners.

'Where are you taking it?' I asked and blanched at his reply.

'Why, Lynn, the Cottage Orphanage, of course – those poor kids in there have nothing. Now, come along, you two, a little drive will do you both good.'

When we arrived at the orphanage he left us sitting in the car, walked up to the front door and handed over the bags. He said nothing more to us, but we understood a threat when we were given one.

When Julia came the next time, it was just Andy and me who greeted her. It was me, I was convinced, that she was more interested in. Some small alarm must have gone off in her head, I just knew it had. The questions she asked were easy enough: they were about homework, school and what friends I had. But that did not stop me feeling that she was searching for something behind my responses to them.

On her third visit, she gave me a card with her phone number on it. 'If you ever need to talk about anything,' she told me, 'just ring. Even if I'm not in the office, you can leave a message.'

I tucked that card away; I did not want my father to see it. It was, I believed, a little piece of security if things really got too bad.

On another visit, Julia talked about clothes. I had outgrown many of mine and what I was wearing was tight, especially over my now developing bust. That was when she told me she had another client, a girl who, though a little older than me, was not much taller. She was, Julia explained, looking to give some of her clothes away. She wanted them to go to someone who would enjoy them. Would I like them?

Of course, I said yes and the next time she came, she was carrying a large suitcase that she opened up, once inside. I thought the clothes were absolutely beautiful.

I asked who the girl was. Julia explained carefully that her clients were confidential so she was not allowed to give out names, but if I wanted to write a thank you note then I could, although she asked me not to put my address on it or sign my name.

Happily, I got out a pen and paper for that task.

I never did find out who the girl was, even though over the next year I had more than one letter to write to her.

When my father first saw the clothes he was far from happy. He muttered something about us not being a charity case. I think Julia must have guessed what his reaction might be, for she made her next visit a little later in the day when he was more likely to be in.

'It's made my client so happy that her clothes have gone to someone who likes them,' she told him. 'In fact, you accepting them is actually doing her a favour.'

'How does that work then?' he asked suspiciously.

Julia lowered her voice a little.

'Let's just say she's not very well. That's all I can tell you.'

I did not then understand the message that she had conveyed to my father. He did, though, and the clothes were never mentioned again.

I never did learn the name of the girl who had been so generous to me. It was a year later when another case of clothes arrived. It was then that my father told me that they were the last I would receive: my unknown friend had died. I still wish I had met her, just once, to say thank you.

Chapter Twenty

The next memory that I examine has never left my mind; it was what happened when Michelle was visiting me. I was then somewhere between thirteen and fourteen. For almost two years my father had been feeding me little measures of alcohol as well as introducing me to cigarettes. It did not take me long to get addicted to the feel of inhaling nicotine deep down in my lungs. As he saw my need for cigarettes growing, he used them as a reward for letting him abuse me.

There were times when he would leave me alone for days, but I always knew my relative peace would not last forever. Then there were times when the abuse was even worse, when he would pin me against the wall while his hands groped and clutched parts of my body. I could smell him then, feel the heat of his body and almost taste his breath as he panted close to my face. Those were the days when I knew there would be bruises. Sometimes, after a visit from Julia, the moment she had gone, he wanted me upstairs so he could have sex with me.

How did I feel over that time? Detached is probably the best way of describing it. I had trained myself to step outside of my body and feel nothing emotionally.

Just after my thirteenth birthday, Julia's visits ceased. Social services had decided that Andy and I were not at risk. They thought our father looked after us well. On her last visit, after she told me this would be her last, Julia still reminded me that I had her card and could contact her at any time.

If her reports had nothing in them to say that our father was not the ideal parent, perhaps her instinct believed the opposite. But like the police, social services needed facts, not gut feelings.

My growing taste for alcohol and my addiction to nicotine was something I was careful to hide from Michelle. It was not so much that I thought she would mind. After all, we were at an age when we experimented with forbidden things, like inhaling on a cigarette pinched from a parent's packet when no one could see us, borrowing make-up, or even once or twice playing hooky from school. Oh, not for a whole day, we were not brave enough for that, just a couple of classes.

It was not the fact that my father didn't allow me to smoke as he was the one who had encouraged that, I just did not want Michelle to know. Though he never let me have more than one drink — a hangover might just have been noticed at school. I brushed my teeth, sucked mints and washed my hair nearly every day, anything to disguise the smell of alcohol and tobacco. The only one apart from my father who knew was Andy. Not that he minded. At fourteen, he helped himself surreptitiously to small amounts of alcohol and smoked quite a few of the cigarettes I had been given.

My father had relented about my friendship with Michelle. She was, he told me, welcome to visit. I knew what the initial reason was: on Julia's weekly visits she seemed very interested in what sort of social life Andy and I had. She told my father in front of me that she was so pleased that I had a close friend, one whose mother made me so welcome in their home. This left him very little choice than to offer the same hospitality to Michelle. He was also aware that if Julia was contacted again, there would be more visits and this was definitely something he wanted to avoid.

'Can Michelle stay over?' I asked one evening. I had two reasons for that request: I wanted to be able to sit in my room upstairs and chat to someone of my own age and escape my father's company. This was something that he hardly ever let me do; he seemed to expect me to be his constant companion. And I wanted to go to bed knowing he would not come near me. He would hardly risk that if I had a friend sleeping over; he had now met both her parents and I was confident he would never do anything out of order that could get back to them.

All four of us had supper that evening. Once it was over, Andy slunk away to his room. He spent as little time with our family as possible now.

'Oh, don't you two disappear as well,' Dad said at the end of the meal. 'I never get to talk to you, Michelle.' An innocent remark on the surface that made me notice how pretty, with her hair loose and wearing a snug-fitting T-shirt, my friend was looking that day. I saw his eyes slide up and down her body and tried to think of an excuse to get her upstairs, away from his stares. But before I could say anything, Michelle, perhaps thinking he was lonely, said brightly, 'Maybe we could watch television with you for a bit? *Top of the Pops* is on, it's my favourite show. Can we watch that with you?'

'Of course,' he said, giving her that charming smile as he crossed over to where the drinks were and poured himself a generous measure.

'Now, you two, seeing it's the weekend and you are both teenagers now, how about a small sherry each?'

Sherry, I thought. It was usually whisky he gave me and sometimes also a glass of red wine. Still, I supposed that sherry might sound more acceptable than a really strong spirit to our visitor, whose parents would never have allowed her any alcohol. Not only did he pour that out for us, he then whipped out a packet of cigarettes as well.

'Lynn and I share a couple just to celebrate it's the weekend,' he told her and with a wide grin, Michelle took one.

'Why, thank you, Mr Morris.'

'Oh, John, please. Being called "Mr" makes me feel like an old man.'

Which you are, I thought, a dirty old man too. Not that I could let those words pass my lips. Anyhow, I was pleased he was being nice to my friend. This was the first time she had stayed over and I wanted her to have a good time. At least he was making an effort; it was very seldom he allowed me to watch *Top of the Pops*.

The three of us moved into the sitting room. Not wanting my father to sit next to me, I sat on one of the armchairs but Michelle, to my dismay, chose to sit on the settee. My father, not needing any more encouragement, sat down next to her.

As soon as our glasses were half-empty, they were topped up, more cigarettes were passed round, while my father asked about the songs being performed. I noticed his face becoming flushed as he swallowed yet another glass of whisky, while Michelle, who had probably never had alcohol before, was giggling at everything he said.

I saw him move closer to her and felt a prickle of unease. Another drink was poured, his voice was beginning to slur. Michelle stopped giggling and looked over in my direction. Her expression told me that she was starting to feel uncomfortable. A charming older man treating her as an equal was one thing, a drunken one slurring away was another. *Top of the Pops* had come to an end and I was just about to make our excuses when the hairs on the back of my neck stood up: he had casually placed a hand on her bare leg and was sliding it upwards.

She suddenly looked very young and scared.

'Got to go, Dad,' I said, jumping up. I quickly picked up the sherry bottle along with his packet of cigarettes. He would have another packet somewhere and we would need both them and the sherry once we got upstairs.

'Come, Michelle,' I said firmly and, taking her by the arm, I pulled her out of the room.

'What was all that about?' she asked.

'Drink,' I said abruptly as I searched for a reasonable excuse she would swallow. 'I think he was so drunk that for just a moment he thought you were my mum. It's just you were sitting next to him, where she always used to sit,' I babbled.

If she repeated any of this to her parents I knew that would be the end of her ever being allowed to put a foot in our house again.

The next morning, I told him the excuse I had made. 'If she tells her father,' I said, 'you could be in big trouble. Giving her cigarettes and alcohol and sticking your hand up her skirt!' Not that it was him I was bothered about, but I could not contemplate losing Michelle's friendship.

He played along with it and when she came nervously into the kitchen he told her how sorry he was: 'It's just that I miss my wife so much,' he explained, a sad hangdog expression on his face, which I knew to be true, 'and I'd had a little too much to drink. It's always worse at the weekends.' Also true. 'Just for a moment I thought it was her sitting next to me. I'm really most embarrassed and desperately sorry, Michelle.' Well, I'm sure he was sorry, but I did not believe for one moment, drunk as he was, that he had thought Michelle was my mother.

Michelle said all the right things but when her eyes met mine, I knew she did not believe him. Later, I asked her not to tell anyone.

'I won't,' she said, patting my arm. 'I just won't sit on that settee again!'

She laughed then and told me to forget it, she already had.

But I knew she hadn't.

Chapter Twenty-One

Just when I thought our lives could not be any worse, my father lost his job. His company had been exceptionally understanding at first, but once Dad had been widowed for over a year, they expected far more than he was giving. Taking too much time off was the reason, or rather, it was the one he gave Andy and me. The thought of him always being in the house was a situation that was almost more than I could bring myself to contemplate. No privacy would be afforded us and no doubt he would still expect to be waited on hand and foot.

If having my father out of work bothered me, it was nothing compared to the devastating effect that the next piece of bad news had. He could not wait to share it and I detected a note of triumph in his voice as he informed us that he had had to let Doris go.

When I asked why he just said that social services would not pay for her while he was unemployed and he certainly could not afford her as he was on benefits: 'So we will all have to pull together, work out a roster or something.' Meaning you and Andy can do just about everything and I will inspect and criticise, I thought.

After dropping those two bombshells he went on to make further excuses for becoming unemployed. He blamed it largely on having to take time off to see to us. My father certainly had a knack for recreating history. Once he had finished giving us his version of why he had been fired, he casually tossed a barbed remark over his shoulder as he walked from the kitchen to the sitting room: 'Sorry, but your easy lives have come to an end.'

That throwaway remark, if it wasn't so ironic, had us almost laughing.

'I wonder which part of our lives he thinks has been so easy?' my brother spluttered in anger and in response, I just shrugged.

The devastating reality of losing Doris was beginning to sink in. It was not the thought of all the extra work I was expected to do – after all, I still did all the washing and quite a lot of the cleaning – it was the idea of losing Doris's company and support that I found the most distressing. She had become the mum I no longer had, or in some ways had never had. I also knew that without her presence in the house, my father would come down on me hard and expect even more housework done. As far as he was concerned, my homework was not important: I was a girl, wasn't I? And girls could get a job in a shop or office without much in the way of qualifications. I had told him I wanted more than that, but he showed little interest.

As if reading my mind, Andy put his arm round my shoulder.

'Come on, Sis, we'll sort something out. I know he thinks he can sit around all day, watching television and waiting for us to come back to make him something to eat, but he'll get bored eventually and start looking for work. He likes money too much to have to live without it, doesn't he? Besides, he won't be able to afford the booze he likes so much.'

'I suppose,' I said, unconvinced he would get smartened up and go job hunting. But trying to put on a brave face, I played along: 'Maybe he'll get one that takes him travelling again. That would be good.'

My brother was right about one thing: our father did sit around all day waiting for us. He was wrong about television, though. Dad found a new hobby: CB radio. He was also wrong about the job hunting.

As far as I know, he never worked again.

Then, we were unaware of just what might pan out for us. And being unaware, we allowed ourselves to fantasise a little optimism for the future.

'Anyway,' Andy said, 'I don't care what he says about me concentrating on my homework and not helping you, I'm going to. So, don't you worry. If he tries to stop you doing your homework, tell him the Head called you in and told you next time you didn't turn in a good effort, she was going to talk to your father. Trust me, Dad would not want that.'

I waited just a few days before I put his plan into action. Not that there was any truth in the story about the Head, for I had too many ambitions for my future, so my homework was always going to get done even if that meant getting up very early in the morning to complete it, which it often did.

'Alright, alright,' was his reply, 'Get your brother to help out. Just do your homework in the kitchen so I can check you're working, not reading some trashy magazine upstairs.'

Round one to us, I told Andy, giving him a high-five. After that small confrontation, Dad no longer appeared to care what we did. As long as the house was kept clean and Andy and I managed to cook up a reasonably decent meal, he took little notice – he was too busy on that CB radio to bother too much with us.

The only part of our roster that had his name on it was the shopping. It did not take long for me to work out that he was getting stingier and stingier on both the quality and the amount of food he brought in.

'I'm on benefits, aren't I?' he snapped when I asked if he could put some fruit on the shopping list. 'If you want fruit, you better get Saturday jobs.'

It was Andy who pointed out that if we did that, who was going to clean and do the washing?

A small portion of fruit came in with the next load of shopping. Which I noticed still included whisky and a cartoon of cigarettes.

When autumn brought with it the first chillier months, my father refused to have the heating switched on. 'Too expensive' was the reason he gave us, while warming himself in front of the lounge's blazing fire. We worked out without saying anything that there was no point in telling him that the rest of the house was freezing.

When the coal looked as though it was running out, we told him he had better order some more. A crafty expression flitted across his face. He had an idea that would get us out of the house on a Saturday and save money as well: 'You two can spend your Saturdays collecting firewood.'

'You mean,' said Andy, 'you don't get extra benefits for Lynn and me that could actually be spent on us just a little, like coming home to a warm house, for instance?'

'Leave it, Andy,' I muttered when I saw Dad's face turning red and knew that it would not take much more for his temper to explode. Anyhow, I knew what he would say for I had heard it enough times: he would tell us how he grew up in a house where there was no washing machine, no vacuum cleaner and no running hot water and certainly no heating, so I had no interest in hearing it all again.

'We'll take the wheelbarrow down to the Foreshore,' I said before Andy could get another word out, 'that's where we can find plenty of wood.' I began to feel a small spurt of excitement. The Foreshore, being in front of the country club and also the beginning of the Yorkshire Wolds National Trail, was a great place to go. Loads of picnickers took advantage of its beauty, so why shouldn't we?

'Come on, Andy,' I said firmly when we were out of our father's earshot. 'It gets us out of the house. We can meet our friends when we are out. Michelle's mother will always make us welcome if we drop in on the way back. It's a bit of freedom, isn't it?'

The following Saturday, we pushed that wheelbarrow all the way to the Foreshore, where we found some discarded old railway sleepers. Once home, we sawed them up into decent-sized logs.

On Sunday, we were back out again. This time a couple of Andy's friends turned up, as did Michelle. She was very popular when she handed over packets of sandwiches as well as soft drinks – 'Mum said you've got to eat if you're out all day,' was all she said.

Pushing the wheelbarrow, collecting the wood and sawing up the big logs was very hard work. It was also a chore that my brother and I began to enjoy. I was at an age when I was shooting up in height, as was Andy. What pleased us more was the significant muscle tone we were both developing. My arms and legs were becoming almost as strong as his.

Chapter Twenty-Two

The summer I turned fourteen, although I didn't know it, was the beginning of things in my life changing for the better, certainly in some ways. I had grown significantly in height, become physically strong, and over that summer I decided that I needed to change 'me' and become stronger in my mind as well as body.

The seeds of that decision were planted when Michelle's mother Maggie invited me to join them on their family holiday in Cornwall.

'It's a camping site, but we rent one of the little cottages, usually the same one every year, and Michelle's room has two beds,' she explained, 'so you can tell your dad it doesn't cost anything to take one extra person.'

'We'll be there when you have your birthday too,' added Michelle with a grin. 'Party time! All you need down there are a costume, shorts and a couple of tops. It's so much warmer in Cornwall than it is here. We can go swimming every day. Come on, Lynn, say you'll come.'

'Try stopping me!' I said with a broad smile. I was almost bursting with excitement at the thought of being included as one of the family.

I waited until we had finished supper before telling my father about the invitation.

'No, I don't think so,' was his answer and my heart sank. 'I can't afford to give you any pocket money and you would need some. So, no, Lynn, the answer is absolutely not.'

I argued and again emphasised that it was not going to cost anything but his face took on that stony expression I knew so well. And with a sinking heart I started to accept that he would not change his mind. Not that I was prepared to let my one opportunity to have some freedom evaporate without a fight.

'So, what did your dad say?' Michelle asked as soon as we saw each other the next morning at school.

'He said no.'

'What?! The miserable old git! He must have given a reason, though. What was it?'

'He said that he couldn't afford to give me any pocket money. I tried telling him that I didn't need any and that he would have less costs with me away and he just went on about how I would have to pay my way. You know, chip in to all the costs.'

'OK, Plan B it is. I'll get both my parents on the case. Maybe we can call round and see him? Don't mention it to him again, let him think you've accepted him not letting you come with us.'

Which was exactly what I did. I just carried on as usual: cooking, cleaning. If he expected sulks, he was not going to get them.

It was just after school had broken up when Michelle and her mother arrived at our house, unannounced.

'Just popping in to invite you all over for a Sunday barbecue,' was the excuse they used. Now this was an invitation my father accepted happily. He had clearly given no more thought to the holiday since he had said no. As far as he was concerned I had accepted that decision so he was not for one moment expecting that the subject would be raised again when we visited.

Once Dad was on his second beer and looking completely relaxed, it was Michelle's father who brought up the subject of the holiday. 'Be good for Michelle to have a friend with her. Being an only child is tough, especially in your teens,' he said almost out of the blue. 'We are really grateful to your daughter. Michelle was not happy about us moving here, she did not want to change schools and leave all her friends behind, but thanks to Lynn, she's made new ones. So, my wife and I would really like to have her with us this holiday. Sometimes there are other kids her age, but it's not guaranteed.'

And that was that. My father, not having a believable excuse tucked up his sleeve, capitulated and even went so far as to thank Michelle's parents for thinking of me.

I thought for a moment that Andy and Michelle were going to burst out laughing. Somehow they managed to restrain themselves and when Dad stood chatting to Michelle's dad at the grill with his back to us, the two of them just gave me the thumbs-up.

That holiday was one of the best experiences of my life. Michelle's father, a stocky man with a receding hairline and a wide, friendly smile, slipped £5 into my hand the moment I got in the car. 'Just so you and Michelle can wander off if you want to and treat yourselves to an ice cream or a cold drink,' he said gruffly when I stammered out my thanks. I even enjoyed the long drive there.

Michelle's parents shared the driving and I got a chance to see much more of the English countryside.

It was noticing even more how a normal family acted around each other that brought home to me just how abnormal ours was. It had never been a home with happiness and laughter inside it. Not when my mother was alive and certainly, despite Grandpa's efforts, not after her death. The only little bit of light in my life was that I was not alone; at least I had Andy.

'Your father's a bully,' Michelle said to me on that holiday. 'You've got to start standing up for yourself, Lynn. Bullies are cowards. Well, that's what my dad says anyway.'

At that time in my life I didn't think standing up for myself was really an option I could exercise but I said I would, just to please her.

A few days into the holiday, I celebrated my fourteenth birthday. The night before, there had been some mention that they would have to do something nice. I thought the holiday and the £5 spending money were the best presents I could have.

In the morning, it was Michelle's boisterous singing of 'Happy Birthday' that woke me. As soon as I sat up, she told me to get up quickly – she had a little surprise for me. But it was more than a little surprise waiting for me in the living area. There was a whole pile of brightly wrapped packages that were, as Michelle put it, waiting for me to unwrap them, plus cards from nearly all my classmates, one from my teacher and cards from Andy and my father.

Michelle must have organised it, I thought, as I read all the messages. They made me feel warm inside. I had never realised how much my classmates thought of me. If I was happy at having so many cards, I gasped with pleasure when I opened my presents, the first one being a watch.

'No excuse for being late again!' said my friend with a smirk, pushing present number two into my hands, a soft cuddly teddy, and lastly, a huge box of chocolates to 'share'.

'And,' said a smiling Maggie as she joined us, 'there's another surprise to look forward to later on. This evening, we're all going out to a really nice restaurant. It's our birthday treat.' And she stood on tiptoes to kiss my cheek.

'Heavens, how tall you've grown, Lynn!'

'Soon be as tall as your dad,' said Michelle and I sensed she meant more by those words than just comparing our heights.

It was during the autumn term that I finally reached the conclusion that enough was enough and it was time to stand up for myself. What angered me about my decision was not that I made it, but how long it took for me to reach a point where I did.

I felt a fury boiling inside me when I was sitting in the classroom with a teacher giving us all a talk about a relatively new organisation called Childline. She explained a little of its history: how TV presenter Esther Rantzen had believed strongly enough in the concept to gain the interest of the BBC. They agreed to set up a trial helpline after a programme on child abuse aired on the BBC as a trial run in 1986. After 50,000 calls were made on just that one night, it was clear how right Esther Rantzen was in her conviction that a helpline for abused children was badly needed. Ever since it was established, the lines had been inundated with thousands of calls. 'Childline,' the teacher said, 'has helped change the lives of thousands of children who thought their situations were hopeless.'

She went on to explain exactly what happens when a child makes a call and emphasised that no child would be in trouble for finding the courage to dial that number. Also, even if it was not about them but another child who had confided their secret to a friend, that call could also be made. She did make it clear that all calls were confidential. That meant the child was protected from the person who was abusing them.

However careful the teacher was being in her talk, it became clear to me that schools and social workers had come to realise that it was not only the children who were taken and found murdered who were the victims of abuse. Since Childline began they had been made even more aware that the abusers could be the same people who turned up at PTA meetings. They could also be family members or friends, neighbours and other people children encountered.

Michelle was the first girl in the class to raise her hand and ask a question.

'What happens to the children where their home life is really bad?' she wanted to know.

'Then, Michelle, they are found a new home, where they will be safe,' was the answer.

'And if there is more than one child?'

'Well, then they will all be found a place where they will be cared for.'

'Together?'

The teacher's long pause before she gave the answer showed me she was not very confident of her assurances. She said she was sure they would stay together 'if possible'. It told me more than if she had answered no, for her answer took too long in coming for me to feel confident in her response.

I did wonder if, after being given far more facts to impart than she actually wanted to share with us, she examined every father who came to the school from there onwards with suspicious eyes. It was while listening to her that I suddenly understood why the social worker Julia had given me her card and how often she had told me I could ring her if I had anything at all that I needed to talk about. She had suspected something was wrong in our house all along, as had Doris. Of course, at the back of my mind I always knew why that suspicion had been aroused: it was the sheets, that's why Doris asked again and again about them having been washed before she came.

I think now that Doris had gone to social services and said that it might be a good idea if a social worker had a closer look at Andy and me. And that was the reason Julia had visited us every week for a year.

How, I asked myself, had I suppressed my desire to ask for help? I knew the answer, it was the fear that my father had instilled in Andy and me since we were small children that had succeeded in keeping us quiet. He had always known he was committing a crime and now I guessed Michelle did as well. I felt hot burning shame at my own weakness. What was happening in our home was not normal. Oh, dear God, I thought in a blind panic, if Michelle had noticed the expression on my face in that class, had anyone else? After all, I was not a little child anymore and still, I allowed my father's actions to continue.

Right, I thought, pull yourself together, Lynn. You're going to put a stop to this.

It was during our main break that Michelle confronted me. She dragged me over to a quiet corner, looked me in the eye and said, 'Your father's been doing it to you, Lynn, hasn't he?'

As she spoke those words I felt the heat rise up in my face. At first I experienced such an overwhelming rush of embarrassment and shame that I could not answer her.

'Don't tell anyone, please, Michelle,' I managed to say. 'Please, I beg you, just let me handle this.'

'I won't say anything, if you promise me something.'

'What?'

'That you will tackle him, say there's been talks at school by the teachers. That they have explained exactly what help is out there. Will you do that, can you promise?'

'Yes, I promise,' I answered, thought it was not just her I was saying that to, I was also telling myself.

'Good! I've always known there was something off about him. My mother doesn't like him either.'

'You've not said anything to her, have you?'

'No, Lynn, I haven't. I only thought he was, but then I saw the expression on your face when our teacher was talking and I knew for sure. Ever since he put his hand on my leg that night, I knew he was a bit of a dirty old man, but that was all. But he's doing a lot more than that, isn't he? Just tell him if he ever comes near you again, you're phoning Childline. That should scare him.'

The rest of that day passed in a blur. My feelings of both shame and anger overwhelmed me, feelings that almost obliterated the fear I had carried for so long. Up until then, I had believed what he had always told us, that Andy and I would be separated and placed in care if I told anyone. Well, I reasoned, Andy was fifteen now, so we would not be apart for long. Would other parents want their children mixing with us if it all came out? We might be victims, but not ones they would want in their lives. Too bad, I decided, we could always move away if that was the case. We would have each other, wouldn't we?

Right, I thought, I will just tackle him, tell him he's a pervert. Threaten to ring Julia. When I left school that day, I scuttled out as fast as I could. Too confused and too embarrassed for any further questions, I did not want to walk with Michelle. I did not want to look in her face and see the pity there, I needed time on my own to think and I just wanted to get home as quickly as possible and plan what I was going to do next. I did not even want to discuss what the teacher had said with Andy although I guessed if our class had been given the information, others would have heard the same talk. No doubt he would bring it up. It was as those thoughts were tumbling around in my head that I heard footsteps behind me. Andy's voice called out for me to wait.

'Where're you off to in such a hurry?'

'Home,' I said. 'Look, Andy, I need to see Dad on my own.'

'You had that talk today, didn't you? We had it yesterday.' Seeing my face, his voice grew more self-assured. 'I knew you would also have it. So, you know all about that organisation that you only have to ring?'

'Yes. Why didn't you tell me about it?'

'I wanted you to hear it all properly. Whatever happens now, it's got to be your decision, Lynn. It's you who has had to put up with him doing things to you for all these years. Because of him it's your life that has been made a misery. I'll back you up though, you know that,' he said, giving my arm a reassuring squeeze. 'Now, are you sure you want to tackle him on your own?'

'Yes, Andy, I'm sure,' I told him, to which he just said, 'OK' and went to his room when we reached the house.

Once I was on my own, my courage started seeping out of me. Just how was I going to handle this, I asked myself. I sat on the settee, my head in my hands, dreading what was going to happen next. I was still sitting there when I heard my father coming in. When he walked into the lounge I could hardly bring myself to look up at him. I could tell he'd been drinking, something that always made me feel uneasy, and what little was left of my courage deserted me. I got off the settee, muttering something about having to change out of my school uniform.

'Now, what's the rush, Lynn? Come here and give your old man a little hug,' he said. He raised his arms and pulled me into them, then lowered one hand and pushed it up between my legs.

'You like this, I know you do,' he told me, his hand moving upwards to my crotch. That was the moment when all the years of anger in me shot to the surface and finally erupted.

'No, I fucking don't!' I screamed in his face and I brought my knee up as hard as I could, between his legs. He grunted in pain and shock and as his head came down, I saw my chance and headbutted him. 'Don't you *ever* touch me like that again, you filthy pervert!' I shouted. As I ran out of the room and up the stairs I could hear him groaning in pain. It felt good and I did not feel any physical pain myself.

Once in the relative safety of my room, I found I could not control the huge gusts of triumphant laughter that flowed out of me and went on so long, they made my sides hurt. Tears streamed from my eyes as with my arms around my stomach, I rocked back and forth in mirth until my laughter finally subsided. Then reality kicked in: what would he do now? He would want revenge, wouldn't he? I would never be allowed to get away with that. He would be livid. I might be strong and almost as tall as him, but I was still no match for his physical strength.

I was too scared to leave my room, suddenly frightened by what he would do. My stomach was rumbling too. Andy and I were supposed to sort out supper and I wondered if my brother had come back into the house yet from his room above the garage.

Then I heard someone coming up the stairs and real panic set in. There was no lock on my door so he could walk straight in.

But he didn't. Instead, he knocked.

'Lynn,' a small pleading voice was saying, 'Lynnie, I'm sorry, forgive me.'

Now it was his turn to feel fear, I realised.

Chapter Twenty-Three

For a few minutes I had the uneasy feeling that my father's pleading voice was another trick, that if I opened the bedroom door, he would just laugh in my face. Maybe he would tell me I wouldn't dare talk, that he would deny he had done anything and say I had no proof. I worried that if he did, my resolve might just disappear; there was only so much courage that I could muster up.

As I pondered what his next move was going to be, I did nothing to acknowledge him. But there was none made, just that whining voice entreating me not to be angry and to come out. And finally, I roused myself, put my shoulders back and told myself this was the beginning of a new me, one intent on fighting back. I opened the door and looked dispassionately into the face of the man outside.

It was over the course of that evening that, with fresh clear eyes, I came to understand that the father who lived in my head was no longer the same one who was sitting opposite me at the table. I had not noticed before how he had aged in such a relatively short time. No longer the man who used to turn heads, his skin that once glowed with health had taken on a greyish pallor and those bright green eyes mentioned by more than one of my mother's friends were now dull and tinged with the redness of broken capillaries. Even his hands were bonier, while his nails, once trimmed weekly, had grown long and were stained yellow with nicotine. I noticed that night how his hands shook when he poured a drink and when he inhaled deeply on his cigarette, his chest wheezed.

This was not a man to be afraid of any longer. Why, I thought suddenly, I'm as strong as him – in fact, I'm probably stronger. And as my father met my eyes I knew that he too recognised his hold over me had withered away.

And what of my big brother? I had always seen Andy as such and looked over at him with the same assessing eyes that had just examined my father. With his bright blue eyes and that untamable hair that, no matter how often it was brushed back, fell over his forehead, I felt a wave of tenderness. At fifteen and sixteen, we looked even more like twins than we had done when small. Ever since Doris had to help me with my hair, I, like my brother, wore it cut short. Both of us had shot up in height. I was now five foot ten inches and I have to admit in pretty good shape; those years of chores had worked better than any expensive gym machinery.

I thought of how, ever since we were small children, Andy had always been there for me, wiped my tears, hugged me when my mother ignored me and thought of different ways to make me happy. When he was still closer to our father, he had followed him about and watched as household jobs were done and small gadgets repaired. Gradually, he picked up how to do it himself. When he was a little older, it was a hobby that began to earn him small amounts of money – money spent more often than not on me rather than himself. Little gifts would appear mysteriously in my room: bars of chocolate, a packet of sweets or new pencils.

I remembered us walking back from school when I was about thirteen. It was a few weeks before Easter and the shops were full of Easter eggs. There was one shop I couldn't help stopping in front of and staring into the beautiful window: the centrepiece was the biggest chocolate bunny I had ever seen.

'Ooh, just look at that, Andy!'

'Mmm, I don't think even my little sister could eat all that chocolate,' he said teasingly.

On Easter morning, he bounced into my room carrying a box. Inside was a chocolate bunny decorated with a pink ribbon around its neck.

'Not quite as big as the one you liked,' he jested as he gave me a kiss on the cheek and wished me a Happy Easter.

Yes, there was a gentle sweetness in my brother.

As I glanced at him, I had this sudden premonition that it would be me who would look after him in the future. I did not understand then the extent of the harm that had been done to him, not by his childhood, but by mine. That was something I only really started to understand over the next few years.

It was not only my father who had changed, the house had too. Over the years since my mother's death, it had lost its freshness. No matter how many times I opened the windows to let in fresh air, the pall of nicotine fumes refused to fly through them. As you sat on the settee or drew the curtains, the fabric gave up the smell of stale cigarette smoke. There were burn marks on the carpet where my father had dropped cigarettes in his dozing late-night state of drunkenness and the pastel fabric sofas that my mother was once so proud of were now in dire need of replacement.

But more than just these physical signs that life in our home was so different, there were few callers and even fewer invitations too. To begin with, our neighbours continued with the invitations to their barbecues and my father had also been invited to a few dinner parties where a spare man was required to make up the numbers, especially when there was a widow or divorcee at the table.

It had not taken long for those invitations to dry up. I didn't, when I was twelve, know why it was, but I learnt some years later. Making an inappropriate pass at the much-younger sister of one of my mother's friends was a transgression they could not accept. Drinking excessively on its own would not have earned complete displeasure, but turning belligerent when drunk was also not what a host wanted.

At first those well-meaning friends and neighbours made excuses for him, called round with casseroles and freshly baked goods and came to see that Andy and I were coping, but then gradually, especially after my grandfather died, they did their best to avoid us. They had done their duty for several months, but they must have said to each other, 'He's becoming a drunk. Lost his job too, I hear,' and in the end they all seemed to agree to wash their hands of us.

I know that because their children, who like us had become teenagers, told us.

My grandmother had also as good as disappeared from our lives. Knowing how unwelcome she was made to feel by him in our house, her visits had grown less and less. Just before I turned fifteen, she told Andy and me that she was moving to a small village not far out of York.

'The house has become too much for me on my own and as for that big garden, I simply can't manage it. I'm going to sell up and stay with my brother and his family. I've even got a little job lined up, I'm going to work in a charity shop. It gets me out of the house and meeting people.' She then said that we would always be welcome visitors, though even as she said it, we all knew that would not happen while we lived under Dad's roof.

Chapter Twenty-Four

I will never forget what that school talk about Childline helped me achieve in my life. What got to me at the time was hearing about those first 50,000 phone calls after the TV show. Just how many children were living the same lives as mine? That was the question that would not leave me. Even more to the point, how many others were still too young to make that call, the ones like me whose abuse started when they were tiny? They were the ones trapped in their fear.

My father had known that day when I defended myself physically that something outside of our home had instilled a new confidence in me. I think that over the next few days he must have heard all about the content of those talks in school from his drinking cronies. I can imagine those men, as they swilled down their beer, bragging about what they would do to any pervert who touched one of their children or grandchildren, or any other child for that matter. Words like 'castrate' and 'bring back the death penalty' would have been bandied about and all of them would have left the pub feeling more macho than when they entered it. Well, all of them that is except for my father, although I'm sure he said all the right things in front of them too.

No, I don't know for sure that's what happened. I wasn't there, of course, but I like to imagine that is how the scenario played out. Certainly, he had heard something that bothered him for he became almost nervous around us, his hectoring voice finally silenced. Nor did he refuse to let us meet up with friends. He even began to give Andy and me pocket money. Not much, but enough to allow us some financial independence.

As soon as the money was in my hands, Michelle and I raided the charity shops. She being, as she told me, an old hand at spotting bargains, knew exactly what brands and labels were the best to buy and which shops had the best choice.

'Doesn't matter if it's too big,' she told me, 'Mum fixes it for me. Sometimes she just takes an old dress and makes me a top out of it.'

I was amazed at what bargains I managed to find with the help of Michelle's expert eye. She told me that shopping in the more affluent areas gave a greater chance of designer clothes and her nimble fingers ran along a row of clothes, feeling the fabrics: 'Touch tells you about the quality of the cloth, Lynn. Good designers use the best.'

As she was raking through those rails in search of pretty tops and dresses, I was on the lookout for more practical garments – jeans and baggy sweaters were my go-to outfits, although Michelle talked me into a few other things. My height was starting to prove a challenge when buying clothes and we hooted with laughter when trousers only came down to my mid-calves.

'You can start a new trend, Lynn.'

Not only was my father acting more like a father should once I had made it clear what would happen if he ever touched me again, he had also begun to allow me more freedom. But he didn't like it, I knew: if anything, he acted as though he was jealous of Andy's and my closeness.

'Always sitting on that settee together and I know you spend hours in his room too. You two not up to anything you shouldn't be, I hope?'

It took a few seconds to understand what he was insinuating. I was so taken aback at first, I could not find the words to express how he made me feel.

'Don't be stupid, Andy's not a pervert like you,' was all I eventually managed to say before I stalked out of the room. He was right about us chatting away and yes, we did stop talking when he entered the room. What he did not know was just how often we sneaked out at night.

Michelle knew about my smoking but the extent of my drinking, where I was downing at least a couple of large whiskys a night, I did try to hide from her. Nor was she initially told too much about another hobby Andy and I had.

Once our father had consumed enough drink to stagger off to bed or to pass out on the sofa, we knew he would not wake until morning and we had started hanging out with the local motorbike gang, whose hobby was riding bikes up and down the old railway lines and the Foreshore late into the night. There was more than one occasion when they were chased by the police.

Andy had been invited by his mate Steve to join the 'Motorbike Club' as he called it. The two had met at infants' school and remained friends throughout. There were some early evenings when Michelle and I also joined them down at the Foreshore.

There, we would smoke cigarettes, drink bottles of beer and feel that we were rebels. Before she went home for her nine o'clock curfew, Michelle made sure she chewed enough gum to remove any trace of tobacco and alcohol.

It was Steve who first joined the gang and Steve who knew about Andy's skill for fixing things. Once the gang saw for themselves how useful he could be, they ignored the fact that he, like Steve, was under the age to have a motorbike licence and allowed him to join their club.

Discarded and written-off motorbikes more like a heap of scrap metal were bought for very little money by the gang. Some were used for spare parts, others laboriously worked on until the engine roared and the bodywork shone. When I first tagged along with Andy, I just watched them racing along those old disused railway lines. And I, like the others, screamed with laughter when the police, probably reacting to complaints of noise, chased them. They must have known, as we did, that driving their small patrol cars they would have little success in catching up with a powerful speeding bike on those old tracks.

It did not take long before I wanted to do more than just watch: I wanted to sling my legs over a bike, open the throttle and take off.

'No way!' was Andy's response when I suggested it. So much for the brother who never could refuse me anything. But I argued my case and said if he did it, why couldn't I? For the first time he remained implacable to my requests.

'Well, let me be on the pillion then,' I begged.

'Not with me you're not,' came his answer.

It did not stop me then asking Matt, one of the older bikers.

'OK, seeing as you're Andy's little sister. Now, here's the deal: if the police make an appearance, I stop the bike and you hop off immediately, promise?'

'Why?'

'Because we fly those bikes, they hardly touch the ground. Any extra weight just slows us down.'

I realised then that it was the thrill of the chase with that spark of danger that they found so exhilarating, though I did wonder why the police even bothered chasing them when they never managed to catch any of the riders. I don't know where the bikes were hidden during the daytime, but it must have been somewhere pretty tucked away, especially as some were unlicenced.

'So, here's your crash helmet,' Matt said later that evening once Michelle had left. 'Put that on, hop on, then wrap your arms tightly around me and hang on tight,' were the only instructions he gave me. It was all I needed. I had watched them enough to know that when the rider leaned over, I had to mirror the angle of lean or I would unsteady the bike or even bring it down. I had never felt anything so exhilarating as tearing along, the wind in my face and my arms tightly wrapped around the biker. It felt like total freedom and from that very first ride, I was hooked and eager to ride a bike of my own.

'Not until you are sixteen,' was all that was said to me.

Of course, I was fully aware that what was going on was, strictly speaking, illegal. Not only were Steve and Andy underage, not every bike had an MOT or insurance. That was why I was keeping the beginning of my new passion a secret from Michelle. I could just imagine what her parents would say if the police turned up at their door. If she knew I was riding pillion, she would want to try it too. As far as she knew, we just watched. Nor did I share with her my passionate dream: to have my own bike.

Chapter Twenty-Five

I can still picture the last Christmas the three of us spent in the house. The season, which everyone else saw as a festive one, was not something that Andy and I were looking forward to. Our house, for I could no longer think of it as a home but just a place where three people lived, had become devoid of both friends and family. There were no festive get-togethers, no grandfather experimenting with his cooking, no Gavin and no mother, and my father was a shadow of the man he had once been.

Even though I was free of his advances, there were times I just wished that the nice father, whom I had seen on more than one occasion, would put in an occasional appearance. I was tired of the one who drowned his sorrows in as much alcohol as he could swallow. No, living there was no one's idea of fun. Still, after a discussion one breakfast time, we all decided to try, that Christmas, to ignore the ghosts that dwelt there and make it as cheerful a time as we could.

'Let's try and make it a decent one this year, Lynn,' Andy suggested. 'I don't want to spend the whole day being depressed and just watching him getting drunk and maudlin, do you?'

'No, I absolutely don't.'

So, we searched out long-forgotten boxes of decorations and a fake pine tree that our parents had bought when we were very little, placed our measly collection of Christmas cards on the mantelpiece and made sure we were well-stocked with logs. Out came the vacuum cleaner, polish and dusters, and between us the place was spring-cleaned from top to bottom. Cold as it was, once my father was out of the house, every window was flung open. Andy even bought some special Christmas spiced potpourri: 'Can't afford flowers, but this will make it smell fresher and more like Christmas,' he said with a wry grin. After we had made the house look as festive as possible, we asked our father for money to go shopping.

'The shops will be empty if we leave it too long,' we told him.

'Oh, don't worry. I've ordered everything, did it some time ago, actually.' A statement that almost made our mouths drop open. 'As your grandmother's not coming this year, there's only going to be the three of us so we're not having a turkey unless you fancy eating it for a week, because I certainly don't. Anyhow, the butcher has put aside a capon, which he tells me is just a very large chicken, some pork sausages ...' and he rattled off a few more things that would be added to the meal. 'I'll give you two a hand with the cooking as well.'

Another first, I thought, and found myself smiling at him. Seeing as he was in such a reasonable mood, I wanted to ask if we could invite Gavin as well. There was more than enough room in the house for him so he could even stay the night. Surely now, after so much time had passed, there wouldn't be any objection? After all, he had done nothing worse than getting on my father's nerves.

But Dad forestalled that request by bringing up his name first.

'One of the reasons your grandmother's not coming this year is because she has invited Gavin to spend Christmas with her and her brother's family so whatever you think, it is not because I didn't invite her. I know she got all uppity because she thought I didn't want her over all the time, but that doesn't mean she isn't welcome here occasionally. Anyhow, she's coming over on New Year's Day, alright?'

I beamed at him then; I really missed my grandmother since she had moved.

There were times when I remembered the charming man my father had been and forgot about everything else. I suppose every child wants to feel loved for if we are unlovable to our parents, what chance do we have of finding love later on in life?

We had all been invited round to Michelle's on Christmas Eve. She thought I was disappointed that the invitation was not for the actual day and took me to one side to explain. Not that I needed to be told. Of course I knew why, something she confirmed with her first couple of sentences.

'Look, Lynn, if we could have just you and Andy over, you know you would be more than welcome.'

'But not my dad, you mean?'

'No. He's not very popular, is he? Most people, my mum and dad included, think he's been a really awful father. I've heard him and my mother saying they don't know why you two were never taken into care. To be honest, my dad can't stand the way he's treated you and Andy, nor can Mum. They're only nice to him for your sake otherwise you'd never be allowed to stay over, would you? But there's another reason too. Dad doesn't trust him when there's drink about – he's heard the stories and knows he can turn nasty. And that would be Christmas spoilt for all of us. We want to see you though and that's why Mum's inviting you over for drinks and a few snacks on Christmas Eve, but Dad's said not too much alcohol is to be offered. Of course, Mum will be diplomatic and tell him that she has her whole family descending on her and she's still got masses of cooking to do that evening and she hardly knows where she's going to put them all. So, is that OK with you? Wish you were coming for Christmas Day, though.'

'Oh, Michelle, you worry too much. I know people don't want him in their homes, hardly anyone comes to see us now. It used to be so different,' I said wistfully, remembering all those parties my parents gave and also went to at this time of year.

'Well, we'll still have a nice time. My parents will make sure of that. And let's make a plan to do something on Boxing Day, alright?'

But instead of phoning Michelle and sneaking out, I got stupidly drunk.

Of course, my father made comments about us not being good enough, now he did not have a top job, to be invited to Michelle's parents for Christmas or even a proper Christmas Eve dinner. He even mentioned how the neighbours had dropped him too.

'Dropped Andy and me as well and only because of you,' I felt like saying but instead, I pressed my lips tightly together to stop the words escaping and ignored his bitter moaning.

'You know it's nothing to do with that, Dad, it's because they have a full house,' I told him. 'So, come on, we're all going to have a nice evening.'

Once we were in Michelle's home, Christmas greetings were exchanged and a bottle of sparkling wine opened. I felt my father relax the minute he downed his first glass. Trays of food were brought out, crackers pulled, and then it was present time.

I gave Michelle a Whitney Houston cassette, *I Wanna Dance with Somebody (Who Loves Me)*, and was rewarded by a squeal of delight. 'Just what I wanted,' she assured me. Andy surprised me as he gave her a silver chain with the letter 'M' dangling from it.

'I know your presents should be wrapped,' said Michelle, 'but sorry, they're not. I want to watch your faces when you see them.'

Fair enough, I thought, completely mystified as to what they might be. Without waiting for a reply, she scuttled over to the settee and brought out two large carrier bags that were hidden behind it. Inside mine was a black velvet jacket.

'Charity shop bargain,' she told me with a grin. 'Will look really good with your jeans and Andy, you're not forgotten, I just knew you would love this,' and a dark brown leather flying jacket with sheepskin cuffs and collar was brought out of the other bag.

'Antique RAF!' she exclaimed excitedly, 'even better than a biker's one. That was a real lucky find. Cool, eh?'

Andy flushed with pleasure as he stuttered out his thanks and without waiting, slipped it on.

'A bit too butch for you, Lynn, or I would have got one for you too.' And there was no mistaking the meaning of the wicked grin she gave me then.

Now it was my turn to blush. Despite my trying to hide it from her, I realised she knew the full extent of my late-night escapades with the moor motorcyclists.

'Now, Lynn, before you try on the jacket, I want you to look at something,' said Maggie. And she in her turn left the room and returned with a blue dress on a matching hanger.

'Found the fabric some time ago,' she told me with one of her warm smiles, 'and I thought the colour would look wonderful on you. Go and try it on and make sure it fits.'

It did. As I looked at my reflection in Michelle's bedroom mirror, I swirled round. All I needed was an occasion to wear it, but I was at that age when I was sure there would be one.

Dad was given a bottle of whisky. Embarrassed, he confessed that he had not got them anything.

'Your company is good enough, John,' said Maggie.

I had to give it to her, she hid her dislike of him pretty well.

Before we left, a tin of homemade mince pies and a large slab of Christmas cake were pressed on us. 'Always bake too much,' Maggie told us, 'you'll be doing me a favour by taking it.' But she didn't have to persuade me; my mouth was watering as her fruit cakes and mince pies were the stuff of legends. Homemade by Maggie definitely outdid any shop-bought bakes. More thanks were given, a few more hugs, and then we made our way home.

'Right, let's have a nightcap. Might as well open my present now, so we can drink to a Happy Christmas,' said my father as soon as we were through our front door.

I heard the sadness in his voice.

Once the three of us were in the lounge, Andy lit the fire as I rustled up some cheese and biscuits. Not that we were hungry after the vast spread Maggie had put out for us, but just because it was Christmas Eve.

'Well, you two, let's have another drink together, shall we?'

But Dad needed no encouragement as he went over to the cabinet and took out three wine glasses and a bottle of red wine, which he divided meticulously equally between them.

That evening, while I sat on the settee next to Andy, was the first time since she had died that my father really talked about my mother. He told us not a day went past without him thinking of her. I felt Andy tense a couple of times and when his arm slid comfortingly around my shoulders, I just hoped nothing would be said to change the atmosphere. For as my father reminisced about how they first met, he seemed to have completely forgotten both Andy and I missed her as well. As of course, I knew, did her first son, and I couldn't help but wonder how Gavin was spending the evening. I pictured him sitting alone in his small flat, remembering all the other Christmases when he had been a part of a family and she was alive. At least he was going to be with our grandmother the following day.

Christmas Day passed pleasantly enough. To my utter surprise my father gave me a CB radio. Even Andy seemed impressed by that. And he was even more impressed when Dad handed him an envelope with £25 in it.

'Couldn't think what to get you, son,' he muttered, 'but I'm sure you can put it towards something you want.'

My present from Andy was a silver chain, similar to Michelle's but with a matching silver bracelet.

The rest of the morning was taken up with Dad showing me how to use his present. Long before we began cooking, I had grasped it and it did not take too long before I found I absolutely loved it. Chatting away to people I had never met, I felt I could be anyone I wanted to be. (In fact, some of the people I met over those airways became friends over time. One of them, named Jon, actually lived in the same town. We spent hours chatting about everything we could think of before we finally met up. Now, a quarter of a century later, he is still a great pal.)

I waited until Andy and I were in the kitchen to ask the question that had been on the tip of my tongue since he had given Michelle her silver chain.

'Where on earth did you get the money from, Andy?'

'What money, Lynn?'

'You know, the presents you bought Michelle and me?' I said, ignoring his mock innocent expression.

'I've been waiting for you to ask that! Knew you'd be curious. Don't worry, it's not stolen. Had a bit of luck, one of those motorbikes we did up turned out to be quite valuable. As it was me who found all the spare parts, I got half the money when it was sold. It was an early Christmas present, they said, so I thought I would share it with you and Michelle. I had to tell Dad, of course, which was a real nuisance. Now he knows about my interest in bikes, he's really started asking questions.

'Anyway, while we're talking about money, I've got a bit of news for you. I got a job in the pizza bar, just part-time. That's regular money coming in, Sis. So, if Dad drinks our pocket money or forgets it, we don't have to worry. Stops us being quite so dependent on him for everything.'

'When do you start?'

'I've got a couple of shifts this week. I know it means you'll be on your own a bit over Christmas, but the manager says it's the best time for good tips. And we need some money of our own coming in, don't we, Lynn? I want to start buying my own bikes to do up, I'm putting all the money Dad's given me towards that.'

He was right, it would be good not to have to rely on our father for everything. And not worry if he was in a good or bad mood when we needed to ask.

The evening that Andy left for his first shift was the one where I allowed myself to get stupidly drunk. I had cooked supper for my father and myself when, as usual, a bottle of wine appeared on the table. He offered me some and, no longer suspicious of where he thought it might lead, I said yes. The subject not just of my mother came up again but also of my grandfather. As we talked, the bottle became empty and another one was opened and my glass filled. Now I felt safe with him, I tossed it back, for those memories were making me sad too.

If I had left it there I might just have made the stairs and fallen into bed, but I didn't. It was me who walked over to the drinks cabinet and me who poured us both a decent-sized whisky. I have no recollection of what happened after that. No memory of falling flat on the floor and none of my father carrying me up to my room. Nor do I have any idea at all of how many drinks I poured. There's a complete blank in my head between me putting that glass up to my lips and waking up the next morning with a pounding head, blurred vision and vomit on my shoulder. I stank alright! Just breathing in that smell made me feel nauseous, forcing me out of bed and into the bathroom: the reflection in the mirror I finally faced after I had chucked up a couple more times was not a pretty sight.

Shower it is, I told myself, stripping off the clothes I had worn the previous evening and throwing them in the laundry bag. It took some time standing under a hot stream of water for my head to clear a little. Think, I told myself, and a dim, blurry picture entered my head of my dad bending over me, asking me if I was alright, but that was all.

He must have got me upstairs somehow, I decided, and it must have been him who threw that blanket over me. Come to think of it, there was a plastic bowl by my bedside. He must have guessed that I would need to throw up. Yes, that's what must have happened, I decided. He left me on the bed fully dressed and then stumbled off to bed too. Oh well, I thought, he was hardly in a position to be angry with me. Not in the state I'd seen him in. Still, that did not stop me from feeling embarrassed.

'Well, you can't hide away all day,' I told myself, 'get dressed and go downstairs. Just brazen it out, act as though nothing happened and remember, he's been worse. Well, perhaps not worse, but just as bad then. Alright, I suppose he's never needed help getting to bed but then he's had a lot of practice in manoeuvring himself out of a pub and finding his way home so in his own home a flight of stairs was hardly likely to be a problem.'

My next step was to find some headache pills, swallow as much water as I could and then pull on some clean clothes. 'Right, here we go,' my inner voice was saying as I squared my shoulders and marched down the stairs.

The first thing I saw as I entered the kitchen was my father's black eye and cut lip.

'What happened to you?' I asked, hoping he was going to say that he had fallen over.

'You mean, how did I get this?' he said, pointing to his lip. And before I could reply, he flung back his head and burst out laughing. 'My God, you're priceless, Lynn. Don't remember a thing, do you?'

I shook my head, thinking I was about to be told something I really did not want to hear.

'You wouldn't listen to me about mixing all that wine with whisky. You blacked out. I tried to wake you. Shook you a bit, threw some cold water over you, but no, you did not stir, not even when I lifted you up and got you up the stairs. And let me tell you, it was no easy task. Anyhow, I managed to get you through your bedroom door. You opened your eyes then, only for a second or two, but it was long enough for you to call me a bastard and punch me. You certainly carry some wallop there, girl. Anyhow, after doing that, you passed out cold again. I just dumped you on the bed and went through to mine. Then, when I woke up this morning and looked in the mirror, I saw what my daughter had done to me!'

'I'm sorry,' I said, feeling my face flush deeply.

'Oh, it's alright. Don't have to worry about you getting into trouble when you're out anymore, do I? You can clearly look after yourself. But Lynn, go easy with the drink. You don't want to end up a drunk, do you?'

That's great, I thought, coming from the man who had not only introduced me to it, but actively encouraged me to drink in the house. After all, even though I knew he did it because he wanted company, I was still underage.

When I told Andy, he managed to say, in between howls of laughter, 'I just wish that I had been there to see it.'

Chapter Twenty-Six

Andy was right to think that Dad was asking far too many questions about the bikers' club. He wanted to know where the bikes came from and who did them up. Luckily, he was unaware that he was quizzing one of the people who had the skill to bring a dead machine back to life. All he had been told was that my brother had come across some spare parts that came in useful and that he had managed to sell them to Matt, the older biker. He said he used that money to pay for Michelle's and my Christmas presents.

Andy tried to avoid answering any questions but Dad just would not let the subject drop. He needed a new interest, he kept saying. He did not have enough money to buy a new bike, so where was the best place to get an old one that needed a bit of doing up?

'Seeing as how I have such a talented son who could help make it look as good as new ...' he kept saying with a smirk. We knew that at least he meant polishing and cleaning, not rebuilding it. Andy shrugged and said he wasn't sure where everyone bought theirs.

After a couple of weeks of dropping hints, Dad decided that he was not going to be put off any longer. He moaned that we were being unhelpful and what he thought had been subtle requests now became direct ones.

'Come on, Andy, stop hiding your light under a bushel! I know you can fix things. I'll give you the money to find a good bike for me. Means you and me can start doing a few things together. What do you think?'

Andy could hardly say it was the worst idea that he had come up with for a long time and it was far too late for any father-and-son bonding to take place. Not that he ever let it slip, either by actions or words, just how much he loathed and despised our father. He had learnt to become adroit at fending off demands disguised as questions.

'There's no stopping him when he wants something, is there?' he sighed half-angrily, half-laughingly. 'He'll have to find one that's in running order, though. I know I can't stop him, but I'm not working for hours on fixing it, that's for sure. Good thing he doesn't think that's something I can do or I'd never hear the end of it. Anyhow, I don't work for free.'

That I knew. Andy had a post office savings account and every week, money that Dad knew nothing about was being salted away carefully. My brother's plan was to put as much aside as possible. The time when I would be old enough to leave home was coming closer and he wanted enough to get us both somewhere decent to live. Another couple of years would do it and then Andy could start his own repair business and get a proper workshop. He wanted to work with bikes, finding the parts that would refurbish old machines and make them fast but safe to ride.

We both underestimated our father's determination to become part of the life we were making for ourselves. There was something about the motorcycle club that drew him in. Although he tried to hide it, there was a growing resentment in him that

Andy and I had an interest that did not involve him. More to the point, that we did not want him to be any part of. We were growing up, no longer were we afraid of him, he had lost his power over us and we were enjoying our small amount of freedom. Having savoured the sweet taste of independence, we did not wish to give it up. We both knew that our father hated how his control over us was slipping, but there must have been a more devious side to him than we had given him credit for. He managed to get, if not overly so, friendly with a couple of the bikers as he sought them out in the pub. Much to our disgust, he was at least accepted.

Worse was to come, though: he got his own bike.

'You're getting that taxed, I hope?' Andy's question was one that Dad did not bother to answer. 'If you're thinking of riding on those old railway tracks with it, you need to know it's illegal. The police keep trying to catch the ones who race on them.'

'Well, have they caught anyone?'

'No, those races don't take place that often. And the police aren't hanging around the Foreshore every night, it's only if they hear of a race that they turn up. And when they do, the bikes are too fast for those little cop cars to catch them. It's just a sort of game to them, really.'

'Well then, what makes you think they would catch me? The lads say my bike is fast.'

'Because he's an inexperienced prat,' my brother told me later. 'Those guys have been on those bikes since they were kids. And they're fit. He's going to be a right liability if he comes down.'

'Well, we can't stop him.'

'No, more's the pity. The stupid, pathetic old git!'

*

Steve and Matt were more tolerant than us. They said no doubt Dad thought a little bit of danger would put some spice back in his life. Andy and I had a different opinion: our father was jealous of any friends I made, especially male ones. I had seen him watching whenever I was chatting with Steve or Matt – he wanted to be around wherever I was.

'Oh, let him have his fun,' said Matt, 'doesn't matter if he comes here. He's not doing any harm, is he? You're not going to race him then, Andy?'

'No, I'm not.'

'Ah! You're worried he might kill himself?'

'No,' my brother said abruptly, but truthfully.

Broken bones or worse and us having to look after him might have worried Andy, but our father breaking his neck didn't matter to him at all, was what he told me. This was something that he believed until it was put to the test.

'Let's hope he gets bored soon, you know how he is,' Andy said more than once but he didn't. To our constant irritation, no sooner had we sat down in our favourite spots than our father, weighted down with beer, would appear. Beer he was happy to share with the club members if that's what it took to make new friends. In a way I felt a little bit sorry for him: a man who once appeared to have everything was now desperate to mix with a group of people half his age or even younger.

On the evenings Michelle joined us, she grinned when she saw Dad arriving.

'Look on the bright side,' she said, 'if he's sat out here drinking beer, he can't say much about what time you get home, can he?'

'Yep, I suppose you're right. Still, I only come here with Andy and he's got that job. I think my dad now comes down here more than me.'

I knew what my father was aiming for: he wanted to wear Andy down until he agreed to a race. He was, I think, consumed with a desire to show his son, who was fast approaching adulthood, that he was still top dog. The other bikers were not particularly concerned about the police, he knew – illegal racing was not considered high up on their lists of serious crimes. It was mainly illegal because it was dangerous more than doing any harm. The only one at risk was the rider as trains had ceased to run on those tracks some years before. Anyhow, they had no way of knowing when a race was due to be run. It's not as though it was a nightly or even a weekly occurrence. There was little reason either to bring them down for spot checks because most of the gang members rode legal bikes. As for drugs, if there were any about, it was mainly the odd joint and even that was very rare.

The races were arranged on nights when the leaders believed that the police were otherwise occupied. Knowing that, Dad kept pestering Andy to race him. The group tried to talk him out of it, pointing out he had never practised on those tracks, explaining that roads and lanes were a very different terrain. Still, my father refused to listen.

'You're just scared your old man's going to run circles round you. That's the problem, isn't it, son?' was one of his mocking jibes.

In the end, Andy capitulated and agreed to race. It was clear that Dad had not listened to the others telling him that to ride those tracks took a certain skill, one his son possessed but he didn't. A small crowd of us watched them set off. Andy opened the throttle and the bike roared. Within seconds, he was flying over those tracks. My heart was in my mouth as I looked on. Unbeknown to any of us, we were not the only ones watching. No sooner had the two bikes set off than the screech of police sirens was heard. This time they were determined to catch a rider – or in this case, two.

They would never have caught Andy, had he been on his own. My brother told me later that the moment he heard the sirens he knew if he speeded up, Dad would do the same and most probably crash the bike. It was a split-second decision and instead of accelerating, Andy slowed down.

The police must have been jubilant when at last they had two offenders within their grasp.

My brother and my father were taken to the police station and charged with racing on those disused tracks, which was illegal. Also, the cc power of the bikes was too high for Andy not to have a licence. After that, they appeared before the magistrate and were fined. A senior policeman then paid us a home visit.

'You know, Mr Murray,' he said coldly, 'if your son was a little younger, I would be recommending he be placed in care, along with your daughter. I'll tell you that you might think riding illegal bikes is just a bit of fun, but if your son hadn't slowed down then you would not be sitting where you are now. He allowed himself to be caught to stop you flying off those tracks. You're supposed to be the adult, try setting an example. This is a small town and gossip has a loud voice here. I don't want anything else to come to my ears, do you understand?'

My father conceded humbly that he did.

I was not fooled, though: I had seen the malevolent expression in his eyes.

How did the police know about that race? This was the question Andy and I asked each other. We both knew it was unlikely to have been a coincidence that they were waiting for it to begin.

It was Matt who told us.

Our father had been in the pub, boasting loudly for all to hear about his new hobby. Not only that, he told everyone how he was going to show his whippersnapper of a son who the real man in the family was. As the police officer had told us, Hessle is a small town and gossip has a large voice. It did not take long for the police to hear about it. As for the day it was going to happen, the landlord, who despised my father, was all too willing to tell them.

Most of the men in the pub were fathers, if not grandfathers. They might all have drunk a little too much, but they were hardworking men who wanted the best for their kids and encouraging them to race on an illegal track was not something they approved of.

There was never any proof as to which person it was who did the talking, but because of it, thanks to Dad and Andy being arrested, the Foreshore was no longer considered a safe place to hang out.

In the three years since Mum's death we had gone from perfect family to a problem one. If my father had been shunned before, he was even more now. The bikers did not want him around anymore. Not only was he a liability, he had gone against their silent code when he pushed Andy into that race.

The gang still continued, though Michelle only came occasionally and there was no more illegal racing on the tracks. This was something both Andy and I missed, although we still went out with them on the trail runs.

Chapter Twenty-Seven

The atmosphere in our home settled down eventually. To begin with, Dad had told Andy that it was his fault we'd had the police round. If he had not slowed down, they would never have caught them.

'No, they would have been too busy putting him in a body bag,' Andy said ruefully when we were alone. But once his moaning was over, he appeared to have forgotten all about it. Meals were eaten together, Andy and I shared the housework and our father carried on drinking.

A few weeks later, we adopted a dog – Judy, a Labrador/collie cross. She had been rescued by a friend of Matt's after she was found locked up in a garage. She was such a gentle dog, but so nervous it was clear that she had been really badly treated. When I first met her, she was all skin and bone. Her owner had been reported, the dog removed and Matt was fostering her. The RSPCA were hoping to find a good permanent home for her.

Matt told us he would have kept her, but he had two other dogs and she just shook whenever one came near.

'She's scared of her own shadow, poor thing,' he said, giving her a reassuring stroke on her head.

But I was hardly listening for it was love at first sight. Liquid brown eyes met mine when I bent down to stroke her. I remembered my grandfather's dog and how he had squirmed with pleasure whenever the backs of his ears were tickled and slowly moved my hand to that special place. A gentle lick of my wrist showed her appreciation.

'I'm going to ask Dad if we can take her,' I told Matt.

'Good luck with that, Lynn,' he muttered.

'I tell you what, Sis, we've got to get him in a good mood, then bring up the question of Judy,' Andy said, giving my arm a squeeze. 'How about I get pizzas in and a bottle of wine? That should help. Then, when he's stuffed his face, we'll ask about having the dog. We'll promise to look after her, he won't have to do a thing and I'll tell him the dog food won't be on the grocery list, I'll buy it all myself. You never know, he might just surprise us and agree.'

As it was the only plan we could come up with, we put it into operation the following night. Dad hummed and hawed for a bit and then said, 'Alright, so long as she's your responsibility and that means any vet's bill too.'

That summer, I was due to turn sixteen. It was also the summer that marked the time both Andy and I entered adulthood. When school broke up for the long summer holidays we had no idea of what was waiting for us just around the corner. We were unaware that few of the plans we had made – going to open-air concerts, meeting friends at barbecues, spending a weekend or two camping – were to come to fruition.

It was only one week into the holidays when our father dropped his bombshell: he had sold the house and was moving to a two-roomed cottage in Hornsea in East Yorkshire. At first, we did not believe him. He was teasing us, we thought for a few moments, it couldn't be true.

'What do you mean, you've sold our home?' Andy exploded. 'We've not seen anyone around here.'

'No, they came when you were at school,' Dad said smugly.

'You could have told us what you were up to,' Andy snapped. 'How are we all going to fit into a two-roomed cottage?'

'We aren't.' Since the moment he said the house was sold, I had been expecting that reply. 'There's not enough room, you and Lynn will have to make other arrangements.'

'But, Dad, I have another year before I finish school. You know I'm doing business studies and Lynn is learning typing and bookkeeping,' my brother told him.

'Oh yes, I know you two think you can set up your own business. Well, it would take a lot more than what you can save working in that pizza place and a few bits of paper, let me tell you. Anyhow, I left school when I was younger than you and it didn't do me any harm. And there's always evening classes.'

His tune had changed, it seemed. I thought of all those hours of homework that Andy had been forced to do.

Andy looked over at me for some support, but I kept silent. I had no intention of giving Dad the satisfaction of exerting any more of his power over us. He must have had this planned for some time. I felt sick at the thought of how I had allowed myself to believe, despite everything, our father cared for us, a belief that had started to regrow over the Christmas that Andy and I had put so much effort in. Even then, he must have had the month of August, barely a week after I had reached sixteen, circled in his mind. Legally, I was old enough to leave both school and home and he knew it. He was free to get rid of us and I was determined neither to challenge him nor to burst into tears.

'Anyhow,' I heard him saying to Andy, 'I'm telling you both now. Gives you time to sort yourselves out. My new place is far too small for all of us so there's nothing more to talk about. And don't look at me like that, Andy. You've turned seventeen and you have a job of sorts, don't you? I'm sure they will give you more shifts and I know you still make extra money fixing things, don't you?'

Andy, his face white with rage, glared at him then grabbed my arm.

'Come on, Lynn, let's just get out of here for a bit – take Judy for a walk.'

I nodded. Any words I wanted to say were trapped behind the hard lump wedged deeply in my throat. In that short time our father had told us about the house he had ripped our dreams for the future into tiny shreds. Both of us needed to pass our exams. What kind of jobs would we be offered without them? And Judy, what was going to happen to her? Those were the thoughts tumbling through my mind as we walked out. But they did not block the sound of our father's last words thrown defiantly towards our retreating backs: 'Anyway, you have a month to get yourselves sorted.'

'Andy, do you think Dad will help us out? I know he did with Gavin,' I said.

'From what I've heard, Lynn, he's in debt up to his neck so I doubt there will be much left once he's sold it,' he told me.

'But still, there must be something. Surely he doesn't expect us to leave home with nothing? I mean, if we ask him for help, that is,' I persisted.

'I don't know, maybe if we begged. But we're not going to, are we?'

'No, I suppose not. But how much do you have saved?'

'Not enough for a deposit on a flat and a couple of months' rent,' he told me dismally. 'Any landlord seeing how young we are would want financial guarantees anyhow, or six months upfront. And I've not got anything like that.'

'So, what are we going to do?'

'Start looking for a job,' was the answer. 'The pizza bar's always looking for people, so I'll talk to them, see if they can give me more shifts. And I'll ask about you as well.'

'And Judy? What's going to happen about her?'

'I don't know,' was his answer but he looked worried. 'One step at a time is all I can think about.'

Neither of us mentioned that we had good friends we could have gone to. Certainly, Michelle's and Steve's parents would have made room for us, at least until we had taken our exams. So, what stopped us? Pride, I think, or perhaps it was stubbornness. It was something we both knew our father expected us to do and we wanted to prove him wrong, show him we were capable of standing on our own two feet and didn't need help.

Andy made a few phone calls later that day when our father was out.

'Good news, Lynn,' he told me, 'the pizza bar will give me some extra evening shifts cos they have a couple of students leaving soon. You can also start working there straight after your birthday. Now, all we have to do is find somewhere to live in Hull. Those weekend evening shifts go on too late to catch trains.'

Although only a ten-minute train ride away, Hull – where the pizza bar was – was such a different place to Hessle. Much bigger and noisier, and suddenly the idea of living there with Andy gave me a twinge of excitement: it was to be my big step towards independence.

It was the manager of the pizza bar who, after hearing Andy's story, rang around for us, said we had jobs and were hardworking, good kids. The trouble was in most people's view, good kids were not looking for accommodation at our ages. Not being a man to give up easily, he eventually found us a place in a hostel. It was for youngsters who were more or less homeless, he told us. But it was another stepping stone towards sorting our lives out.

'That will do for now, Sis. We'll save up and get something better soon, you'll see,' Andy told me.

The next hurdle was persuading our father to look after Judy. This time I was not far off begging. I simply could not bear the thought of losing her. She had been my companion for only a short time, but to me she was more than a dog: she was the one I could show love to, whisper all my problems into her soft ears and receive loving licks in return.

'Please, Dad,' I forced myself to say when I saw him opening his mouth to refuse, 'call it my sixteenth birthday present. That's all I want. As soon as we get somewhere better to live, I'll fetch her, I promise. It will only be for a few weeks.'

For a split second I thought I caught a glimpse of sadness in his face before he said, 'Oh well, that's alright then.' And I breathed a sigh of utter relief.

More rules were laid down. I was to give him money for her food, he told me, naming an amount higher than the real cost would have been. And I was to visit her at least once a week, but he would exercise her once a day.

That was one hurdle over, I told myself, and very soon I would be in charge of my own life. Then I wouldn't ever have to ask any favours of him again.

Chapter Twenty-Eight

Once I began working, we felt almost rich with having two incomes coming in. After a few weeks where we took as many shifts as we could, we made countless phone calls, trying to find somewhere to rent where we could have Judy. Andy was right about landlords: after taking one look at our youthful faces, the agencies we visited confirmed what he had thought. Without better references than we had, plus a parental guarantee, landlords would not be interested in us. If we wanted to have an animal, an even larger deposit would be requested, they added.

It was one of the girls who worked with us who told us about two bedsitters that were coming up in the block that Julia, a friend of hers, managed. In the end, after meeting Julia, who told us that the landlord was never there and she loved dogs, we decided to settle for them. This was especially ideal as Julia, who had the larger garden flat, offered to dog-sit when we worked late shifts.

'Can't have a dog barking all night,' she said. 'I'd get the complaints and you would get thrown out.'

I couldn't wait to go to Dad's and collect Judy. With the money we had made in tips that week, Andy and I went on a shopping spree in the local pet shop. Into our basket, as well as packets of dog food, went chewy treats, a huge leather bone, a dark blue collar with matching lead and an enormous cushioned bed decorated with paw prints for her to lie on. After all that was deposited in my room, we walked to the station and caught the train to Hornsea.

I was simply brimming over with excitement for the whole of that journey, imagining my dog rushing out to greet me. Because of all the overtime we had put in, it had been two weeks since I had last seen her and I just couldn't wait.

'Aren't you looking forward to seeing her too?' I asked Andy, who was spending his time looking out of the window.

'Of course I am, Lynn, it's Dad I don't want to see. We'll have to stay a bit, I suppose, and I've nothing left to say to him.'

'Don't worry, I'll go on my own next time.'

'Don't know why you would want to, once you have Judy, not after everything he's done.'

I couldn't explain either, not even to myself. Not then, though I can now. For at sixteen, I still had not rid myself of wanting to believe that my parents had cared for me.

Once off that train, I grabbed Andy's arm and walked as fast as I could to where our father's cottage was. As I knocked on the door I was expecting to hear Judy bark, but only silence greeted us. A couple more sharp knocks resulted in the sound of shuffling feet and a key turning in the lock before Dad opened the door.

Unshaven and very pale, he looked even worse than he had just two weeks earlier.

'Lynn, I wasn't expecting you,' were his opening words as I waited for him to step aside and let us in.

'I've come for Judy, Dad. Said I would, I can take her off your hands now.'

Still, he did not invite us in. Something was wrong, I could tell.

'Dad, where is she? Where's Judy?'

'Had to get rid of her, didn't I? You've not been to see me for over two weeks. I had to do all that moving on my own. Got too much for me, thought you'd forgotten about her, so I took her to the PDSA.'

'Where?' I almost screamed.

'In Hessle. Anyway, you should have come. They've probably put her down by now.'

It was Andy who took hold of me, stopping me from flying at him.

'Don't, Lynn, let's just go,' he told me. He wrapped his arm round me and turned to Dad.

'You know what? You're going to die a sad, lonely old man. No one will miss you when you're gone. You've not family now, no friends either, from what I've heard. Neither of us ever wants to set eyes on you again. In fact, you did us a favour, telling us to leave.'

I heard Dad trying to say sorry and calling out to us, asking why we didn't come in as we walked away.

I did not look back.

Andy did his very best to comfort me; he would contact the PDSA and try to find out more.

'I'll phone as soon as we get back,' he promised. 'Lynn, listen to me,' he pleaded when I did not respond. 'I know they don't put dogs down immediately. It's a last resort and one that they don't do willingly, especially with such a lovely and friendly one like Judy. She's the sort of pet that any family with children would love to have, so don't take any notice of what Dad said. He's just trying to upset us. Didn't expect you and me to really be able to get jobs and find somewhere to live. Thought we'd have to ask friends to take us in. That's the reason why he tried to wind you up.'

'I suppose you're right,' I conceded, though I was not totally convinced.

'I know it's a nuisance but I've got to work tonight. If I could swap shifts, I would, but it's too late now. You sure you'll be alright?' he added.

I told him of course I would be fine and that I just wanted a quiet evening in. What I really meant was I wanted to close the door of my room behind me and bawl my eyes out.

I leant my head against the train window as my brother continued talking. Everything he was saying simply went over my head. I knew he would ring as soon as we got back to Hull, not that I had any hope that anything was going to work out. I recognised the sinking feeling in the pit of my stomach as being the same as the one I had when our mother went to the hospital for the last time. Whatever happened, I was not going to see Judy again, I just knew.

As soon as we reached the station Andy marched purposely to the row of telephone boxes. I shook my head when he asked me to come with him, unable to bring myself to stand next to him and hear what was being said. I was frightened I would hear him being given the news that our father was right and Judy had been put down.

As soon as I saw the receiver being placed back and Andy turning towards me, I knew by his expression that something had happened that I would not want to hear.

The good news was that he was right: Judy had not been put down. Instead, she had been found a new home in the countryside. The woman at the PDSA had told him she had gone to a lovely couple who had two sons aged ten and eleven. Like me, they had fallen in love with her straight away.

'I feel better now,' my brother said, 'don't you, Lynn? There's no way she's not being cared for.'

His words, that were supposed to make me feel better, just made me angry. I could not bring myself to answer him; instead, I started walking as fast as I could out of the station. I heard him saying that he thought I would be pleased for her. I knew he was right, that I should have been. I wasn't, though – I just wanted her back.

'Come on, Lynn. She's alive and being loved and looked after. You know, much as I'll miss her too, maybe it's for the best.' He linked his arm through mine. 'It would not have been much of a life for her, living in our bedsits, now would it?'

That might have been true but it did not console me. I gave him a dirty look before opening the door to my room. Once inside, all I could see was the big cushion with the paw prints. My knees buckled and I fell down on it, tears raining down my face.

I had never really felt completely alone, but that day I did. Oh, I knew I had Andy and that he gave me all the support he could, but it was not always enough. What I really wanted, I realised, was to be part of a family. The people I had met who lived in the block still referred to their parents' houses as 'home'. It was where they went when they needed to rest, recover from a broken love affair, or had just woken up one morning, missing their family. When they returned, they brought back little things to brighten their room: packets of food and a bag full of their clean washing, all ironed and folded up by a loving mother. And that was what I wanted too.

When I had Judy, she made me feel that we were a family – Andy, me and our dog. But then I was only sixteen. There is a reason why we are called teenagers at that age: it means we are really somewhere between leaving childhood and becoming an adult. That evening, I reverted to being a child, a very lost and unhappy one. Practically homeless, I missed both my mother and grandfather and wanted to be in a place where I was loved and cared for. However bad our life in the house had been, I just wished I could go back in time to when our father was successful and our mother and grandfather were still alive. Most of all, I missed Judy. I had loved her and then she too had been taken from me. I picked up a glass, filled it with sherry and, wishing there was someone who would comfort me, I wrapped my arms round my knees and rocked myself backwards and forwards.

Alcohol, I found, does not cheer up a depressed person. In fact, if anything, it has completely the opposite effect. By the time I was halfway through the bottle, I was drowning in self-pity. As far as I was concerned, apart from Andy, I had lost everything I loved. From the courses I was doing at school to the friends I had in Hessle, to my mother's and grandfather's deaths. The loss of Judy was the last straw. I could not even face meeting up with Michelle and seeing the pity in her eyes.

At sixteen, I decided there was nothing left to live for.

I stumbled over to where I kept the headache pills, finding nearly a full bottle. That should do it, I said to myself, cramming handfuls into my mouth before washing them down with the remaining sherry. Thankfully, I had not bought any whisky for that combination might just have finished me off.

It was Andy who found me passed out cold when he returned from work and came to check up on me. He phoned for an ambulance.

I was kept in for a day. I told the doctor that I had not meant to take so many pills, insisting I only wanted to sleep, not die. Having assured the medical staff that I would never do anything so stupid again, I was released into Michelle's mother's care. My brother had not known who else to turn to after he found me and had contacted Maggie.

'You,' she told me firmly, 'are going to stay with us for a few days and we'll get you sorted out. No argument.'

Too weak to protest, I followed her out of the ward meekly.

Chapter Twenty-Nine

When I was a child it was Andy who was my salvation, even though I knew from a very early age that he was the one our mother loved the most. Funnily enough, I felt no resentment at knowing that. Instead, I only felt sadness. The memory of the times I tried to hug her and was pushed aside has never left me. Nor has her reply to the question I asked, 'Do you love Andy more than me?'

I felt the sadness in her when she answered, 'He needs me more, but your daddy loves you best.'

At sixteen, I wished I could have asked her whether she knew what his love meant. Said to her, did you did not hear my sobs and screams, see the fear on my face, watch his jealousy, for that was what it was when I dared to ignore him and chattered to my brother. Or did you see me, your four-, five- and six-year-old child, as your rival?

Yes, I wished then that it was not too late to ask her those questions. Now, twenty-five years later, I still don't have the answers.

If only it were possible to meet her one more time. Then she would meet the person I have become: a woman finally content with her life. Yes, I would like it if she could see how I'm surrounded by friends and my small family. Would she be happy for me? Would that rid her of some of the guilt she must have felt? Even now, if I believed she didn't feel any guilt, that would be almost too much to bear. Or maybe she would ask who had helped me place my feet in the right direction.

There had to be someone, surely?

Yes, there was: her name is Elizabeth.

She was the one who, over several months, I unburdened myself to; the one who watched my progress, and in the course of time became my friend. I met her when my world was very dark, after that suicide attempt. It was Maggie who persuaded me to attend group therapy. How much did she know or guess? I never asked and she never told me. All I know is that the group was made up mainly of young people and most of them had been abused one way or another.

I met Elizabeth there. Not that she ever spoke out about her own past. Unlike the others who wanted to talk ceaselessly about the harm done to them, harm by fathers, uncles, stepfathers and even brothers. She was always silent. I was as well, for I felt if I opened up, I would let even more pain in. Both the group and the counsellor knew I had been abused, but that was all. After a few weeks, it was she who approached me.

'Why do you come here?' I asked, for she was not a young woman, nor did she seem troubled. If anything, she appeared not only composed but serene and at peace with herself.

'Sometimes,' she told me, 'there is someone at these meetings who I feel drawn to. Someone I feel I can help.'

'And that's why you come?'

'Yes.'

I did not ask her if I was one of the people she felt such a connection with. One glance into her calm blue eyes gave me that answer. I smiled for the first time since I had walked through the door into the therapy session. Recognising my need, she gently took my hand in hers. I can still see that hand, with its small, delicate bones that belied the strength of her grip whenever I tried to withdraw from her firm grasp.

'Listen to me, Lynn,' she said in a tone that broke through all my resistance. 'I too was abused. Sadly, far too many children are. But back then, when I was even younger than you, it was never talked about, so I believed I was the only one. I blamed myself for it – there must be something wrong with me was what I thought. I convinced myself that in some way I deserved the treatment I endured.

'I left home at fourteen. Ran away and found a job living in, chambermaid work. At first, I made friends and believed I could live the same lives as they did – go to dances and parties, drink a little and have fun. But that entailed meeting boys, and boys, I discovered, wanted the same thing as the man who had abused me.'

'So,' I asked, 'what did you do?'

'I found another job as an au pair. Children, after all, did not pose any threat to me. And that is what I did with my life: I looked after other people's children. And once the children grew and no longer needed me, I left. Oh, the parents always asked me to keep in touch. They told me I was part of their family, but I knew I wasn't. Once out of their door, I walked away.'

'But why, Elizabeth?' I asked.

'I thought then that the children's parents did not know me, not who I really was. They only knew the reliable nanny who looked after their children. They never thought to ask about my family or what I did on my day off, so when I left, I saw no point in keeping in touch. That is what I believed then. Today, everything has changed. Now there is counselling for the abused. It's even permissible to talk about it freely. The world we live in understands that the children are innocent, but not back then, not when I was young.

'Then people saw it as the child's fault and should what happened in the house ever become public knowledge, it was the victim more than the perpetrator who was ostracised. Backs would be turned and her childhood friends forbidden to have anything to do with her. Or if she tried to confide in an adult, she was accused of making up filthy stories and threatened with being incarcerated in the nearest mental hospital.'

'Is that what happened to you?'

'Yes, not all of it, but most. I told an aunt, one who was young and kind, or so I believed. She went straight to my mother. I was beaten and my mouth washed out with soap. Worse came. As I have learnt, a secret is only for one person to know. The moment it is shared, then it is no longer a secret. My aunt told her husband, who had little time for my father, so one night down the pub, he told another, who in turn told several others and eventually it made its way into the ears of the police. My father was questioned, everything denied. "If you repeat those lies," my mother told me, "it's the mental hospital for you. You'll never see us again."

'You know, Lynn, not one person who heard that story asked me if it was true. Instead, parents warned their children not to talk to me. Invitations to their houses stopped. So, at the time in our lives when friendships that can last a lifetime are made, they are denied people like us. When I left home, there was not one person I kept in touch with and that habit has stayed.

'Now those who have never been abused think that children who are want to be taken from their parents, but you and I know that is not so, don't we? What we want is love. That knot which lies heavily in our stomach is not formed by fear, it is grief – grief for the love we ached for that was never shown. That's the truth for you, isn't it, Lynn?'

'Yes,' I whispered.

'Only you can work out how to rid yourself of that ache. But comfort yourself with this thought, that nothing was ever your fault. Once you accept that, you will find your life will become easier. Now, can you tell me a little more?' Elizabeth asked.

I spoke then, not just of my parents and Andy, but of Gavin as well. I had come to understand how unhappy he must have been, I told her.

'Andy and I always thought he was such a bully when we were growing up, we wanted nothing to do with him.'

'And now?'

'I've not seen him since my father threw him out. I could have, I suppose, but something stopped me.'

'Don't put seeing him off,' Elizabeth said firmly. 'Make contact with him – he is family, after all. I'm going to explain to you why having family in your life is important. Without our family, we are rootless people. Maybe that does not matter when we are young, but one day we will feel the loss. And family, my dear, does not have to share the same genes as you. It can be the people we choose and who in their turn choose us so we should always keep in touch, value them and those like Gavin who we have lost along the way, we must find a way to invite back in. Believe me, it's important. I know that now, it is never too late.'

I thought immediately about my once close friendship with Michelle. When we had been forced to leave the area and get jobs she continued with her studies and was well on the way to getting her A-levels and going to university. We hadn't spoken for a while even though Maggie would have kept her up to date with my escapade with the pills.

The one other good thing that came out of that suicide attempt, apart from meeting Elizabeth, of course, was finding out just how many friends I really had and being reconnected with Michelle. It was as if they appeared out of the woodwork once they heard what I had done. There I was, swamped in depression, feeling sorry for myself and not giving a thought to the people who cared for me. It made me understand what Elizabeth meant when she told me that a family does not have to share the same genes.

Anyhow, I told myself, I do have some family. Not only was there my grandmother and Andy, but there was also Gavin. And had I given him much thought over the years? No. It was then I decided that I would go and visit him. Whatever had happened between us when we were younger had been partly resolved during his last year with us.

It only took a couple of phone calls to my grandmother and a week of plucking up courage and then I made the short trip to where Gavin lived.

I wondered what reception I would be given. The door slammed in my face? There had certainly been no love lost between us during most of my childhood. Still, I wanted to at least give it a try. After all, he was my older brother, even if we had different fathers, and neither of us had been shown any kindness by either of ours.

When he opened the door, I saw a heavy young man, unshaven, and who looked uncared for. For a second or two he looked bemused – after all, he had not seen me for several years. As it dawned on him who I was, his round face lit up.

'Thought I would pay you a visit,' I said.

I can't remember now what we talked about at first, and we were both a little awkward together. I remember he offered to make tea and my response: 'Do I need to watch what goes in it?' I asked with a grin. Now the ice was broken.

It was some time after that, when we had met a couple more times, that I told him I had come to understand the hurt he must have felt when our mother appeared to have turned against him, or rather gave the impression that all her love was reserved for her new family. It was then that he told me what his life had been like when she separated from her first husband.

'My father, who as you know was hardly ever mentioned, well, let's just say, I was quite pleased when he left. There were always such terrible rows in the house. My mother crying, saying he did not appreciate her. And he hit me, called me stupid. Said I was not right in the head. He even accused my mother of having an affair because he did not believe I was his. So, after all that, maybe he was right about my head. I mean, why did I wait every weekend, hoping he would come to take me out?'

'To prove you meant something to him,' I suggested. 'You were still a little boy, children find it very hard to take rejection.'

'Yes, I suppose. I got over it and after a while I was happy. My mother and I – well, I thought we were really close. She kept telling me that I was her little companion and wasn't it lovely not to have to listen to any more rows? She said it was just her and me against the world and I believed her. And for a while we did do everything together. She took me to the cinema quite a bit. Of course, we could only go to films that they allowed children into. And then a little later, she made friends with another single mum. She had a kid named Freddy who was about my age and she usually brought him along with her. We had some fun then. It was one of those really hot summers. All four of us would have picnics on the lawn, shower under the water hoses and laugh when we got drenched. That's what I remember the most about then, our mother laughing. Yes, I was happy then. And then your dad came.'

'And what was that like? I mean, him coming into your little world of two?'

'Oh, at first I liked him. I suppose he made sure of that. He took us to the zoo, set up the barbecue at my mother's and even tried playing some ball games with me. You know, when he told me he was going to be my new dad, I was really happy. Well, we did have a couple of great days out and I suppose I thought that was how life was going to be once my mum moved in with him.'

Gavin looked a little sad when he told me the best day ever was when my father had taken them all – my mother, her friend and both children – to the fair. How they had all screamed with laughter at the rides on the bumper cars and with fright on the roller coaster. Afterwards, they had walked around eating ice cream and candy floss and got sunburnt and ended up with a fish and chip supper before returning home.

'Then there was the wedding,' he said. 'It was soon after that though that things changed. My mother stopped calling me her little companion for one thing. In fact, she ignored me a lot of the time. I think that started when she knew she was pregnant. The moment Andy was born, she pushed me aside even more. I know he was a beautiful baby, everyone who came to the house said that. Just like his dad, they kept saying, and she sat there preening as though she had done something wonderful. And then a year later, you arrived and that was that. Now she had two perfect children and no room in her life for one who wasn't. I mean, I was clumsy and no good at sports. In fact, not that much good at school either.'

'Well, you were pretty good at painting and drawing,' I said, glancing at the framed pictures that hung on the wall. 'They are really beautiful,' I told him.

'She didn't think so though,' he said and I heard an echo of his childhood sadness in his voice. And I thought then how terrible it was that all the joy in his life had been sucked out by the time he was ten.

I wonder how long it took for Gavin to realise that our mother had married a man who only pretended to like her first-born son. It was she he wanted, not him. And my father did not waste any time making sure she produced his replacement.

'When did you know what sort of man he was?' I asked.

'It took a while,' he told me and went on to explain that to begin with, he had blamed himself for my father's change in attitude towards him. And then the blame shifted to Andy when he was born and then of course, it incorporated me. It took a while for him to realise that he was not even liked.

'Your father's eyes changed,' his voice became bitter as he recalled his memories, 'they went flat, not just when I tried to get his attention, but even when I walked into a room. I knew then that all the friendliness he had once shown me was just part of an act he put on for Mum. You're trying to think of an excuse for her, but no, I might have blamed you both, but let's face it, Lynn, she stopped loving me before that.'

And when, I silently asked myself, did she cease to love me?

Chapter Thirty

I carried on working at the pizza bar, my only complaint being that my clothes were perfumed with the scent of cooking, cigarette smoke and sweet drinks.

It was nearly eighteen months after we had moved to Hull that I met the man I was to spend the next twelve years with. Not that I had been thinking of meeting anyone when I had gone out with a group of girlfriends. I was content not having a boyfriend. There had been a few boys who I had met in bars and I had made the mistake of letting a couple of them come up to my room. To have a drink, chat and listen to music was what they had said, silly me for believing that. It had not taken long, once they were through the door, to discover that was far from what they had on their mind. Their friendliness disappeared the moment I had let them know that crawling into bed with them was simply not going to happen. Words like 'prick-tease' and worse were thrown at me when I opened the door and told them to get out. Luckily, those years of chopping wood had paid off and made me look quite strong; they must have sensed I was not to be messed with. So that night, meeting a boy was the very last thing on my mind.

We had all gone bar hopping, mixed our drinks and reached the stage of wobbly legs and unrestrained bursts of senseless giggles. It was my suggestion that bags of chips might be a good idea. 'Might just sober us up a bit,' I mentioned, not that my friends seemed to feel the need for that.

'Later, Lynn, let's stop off for one more drink,' they said as, holding each other up, they dived into yet another bar. Another one was not a good idea, I decided. I had a morning shift the next day and after shouting my goodbyes, I weaved my way over to the chip shop.

It was on the way back to the bedsit that I took a short cut, tried to step over a low wall and tripped and fell over. Cursing under my breath, I scrambled up, thankful the bag of chips was still safely in my hand, unscathed. Then I heard a chuckle behind me.

'I'm impressed,' I heard a male voice say.

Turning, I saw a tall, sandy-haired young man smiling at me. That was the start, not of what my friends thought of as a big romance, but a friendship that became nearly as close as Andy's and mine. He told me his name was Jake, sat on the wall with me, passed me his handkerchief for my bloodied knees and helped himself to a couple of chips before walking me back to my flat. But he did not suggest coming in: 'Just want to make sure you are home safe,' was what he told me, before leaving me at the front door. The next night, he turned up at the pizza bar.

From the moment I met him, I felt he was different from the other boys I had met, although I needed proof of that. The mistrust I felt for men was still embedded deep inside me. So, almost straight away, I introduced him to Andy. To my relief the two of them really hit it off.

'Nice guy that, I like him,' was what my brother said, which I understood to mean he approved of Jake and so I started to feel as if I could trust him.

After we had met up several times, I told him a little about my past. Not all of it, but enough for him to put the pieces together. His reaction was to pull me close and whisper nothing like that would ever happen to me again, not while he was around.

He cares for me, I thought, feeling myself totally relax as the warmth ran through me.

Later, I shared my dream: how I wanted to live in the country, keep pets and grow my own fruit and vegetables. Be self-sufficient, I told him, and live off the land. What I didn't know at the time was what I really wanted was to be safe, away from a large town where the boys I met only wanted the same as my father. He said he had a similar ambition and that he too loved the countryside, but first, he had to put more money aside.

On our evenings off, often it was the three of us, him, Andy and I, who hung out together. I cooked meals on the hot plate in my bedsitter and they organised the beer. Occasionally, Gavin was coaxed out of his flat to join us as well. I was happy that we all got on so well. Andy and Gavin had also dropped the past animosities and now I felt as if I had three big brothers.

Come the summer, the three of us took off. 'We can see England and earn money at the same time,' was how Jake described the road trip we were about to embark on. We went fruit picking in Kent, worked on a farm in Devon and then turned around and made our way to Brighton. Andy and Jake found bar work and I got a job in a care home.

In 1990, we decided to make the journey back up to the North just after Christmas. Luck was in for Andy and me: the pizza bar needed staff, while Jake found work on a farm. I had once told him that the only thing missing in my life was a dog, but now I understood that bedsitter land was hardly the right place to bring one up.

'We'll share one then,' he told me. And on my next free day he would take me for a drive.

'Where to?' I asked.

'You'll know when we get there,' he told me and I knew there was no point in asking any more questions. The drive ended at the house of a friend whose Staffy had given birth to five plump, wriggling pups. 'This little one, I think,' said Jake, placing the only female of the litter in my arms. 'Like her?'

I could feel the smile I gave him stretching my face.

'I love her,' I said, holding her to my heart and planting kisses on the top of her soft head.

It was not long before the puppy, who I had already named Zelda, was deemed old enough to leave her mother. Then another drive into the country was arranged. I wondered where we would end up this time.

'There's a beautiful village I'm taking us to,' was all Jake told me once I was in the car. 'There's a nature reserve where we could walk and a great pub to have lunch in. Thought you would enjoy exploring it.'

He was right. Eastrington, situated in the East Riding of Yorkshire, was one of those villages that I would have expected to see on a postcard. We drove past the ponds it was famous for, then down a narrow country lane until we came to a small, grey stone house, where we pulled up.

'Come and have a look,' said Jake, smiling gleefully. Taking me by the hand, he led me along the path of an overgrown garden and into the house. I saw a black stove in the kitchen with a pile of logs beside it, a small oak-beamed sitting room with low ceilings, and through the window, I caught a glimpse of a large back garden with an apple tree in full blossom at the far end of it.

'It's ours if we want it,' he told me and I could hardly speak. It was as though I had gone to sleep and walked into my dream. He explained it came with his new job, which was managing the farm. There was some part-time work for me as well: helping sort out the fruit, vegetables and eggs for the weekly farmers' market.

'Do you like it, Lynn?' he wanted to know and for the first time I heard a little nervousness in his voice.

Of course I did, it was everything I had dreamt of. Two weeks later, we moved in. I looked after the vegetable garden and picked fruit while in his free time, Jake fenced off a section of the garden for us to keep our own hens. We adopted another puppy, a border collie this time. With his dark, intelligent eyes and a tail that never stayed still, he reminded me of my old dog Judy. I named him Jed.

For a long time I was content except for one thing – well, one major thing – my relationship with Jake. When we first met, I felt my life was fulfilling. I had not wanted to change, or even considered changing how things were between us. I had not even expected them to change when we moved into the country and set up home together, but over the years my feelings for him had changed and I believed he felt the same. In many ways, he acted as though we were a couple – he was undoubtedly possessive, glaring at any man who looked at me, and made sure his arm was around my waist or shoulders when I met my friends. Those actions conveyed the message 'She's mine'. Yet, apart from hugs and cuddles, he had never expressed any desire to take our relationship further and I could not bring myself to ask why.

So, I tried in little ways to make him feel he could. I cooked food he liked, sprayed myself with perfume and changed into something pretty when he came back from work, but nothing happened. Nor, I knew, was he interested in anyone else.

Up until then, not only had I never been able to have sex, I had no interest in trying. Kisses and fumbling, yes, but the moment a hand slipped down below my waist, my body would go rigid. When I heard friends talking about their affairs or even their one-night stands, I nodded my head and grinned, as though I got up to exactly the same thing. Of course, I didn't. But Jake was different – I felt I could rely on him, everything told me he would be gentle with me.

In the end it was me who made the first approach and to my chagrin, it was he who rejected it. He liked things the way we were, he told me. But I no longer did. For a long time I hid those feelings, not just from him but from myself as well. In a way I thought that desiring sex was something shameful.

It was while living with Jake that I met the second man in my life: Graham, a sales manager. Somewhere in his late twenties, he was an unassuming character of average height and, with his mouse-brown hair and round face, of average looks. To begin with, I was not in the least bit interested. In fact, I was irritated that he made excuses to call round whenever he knew Jake was at work.

'You have a girlfriend,' I told him when he let me know his intentions. 'And I, in case you haven't noticed, am with Jake.'

'I know,' he told me, looking embarrassed, 'just can't help myself.'

There must have been some village gossip that reached his girlfriend's ears because she managed to turn up at the cottage when he was still on my doorstep. And she tackled me, not him, saying I could get anyone I wanted, so why couldn't I leave her boyfriend alone? It was pointless me telling her that it was him, not me, who was at fault. After Jake's dismissal of my advances, my confidence was at a very low ebb, so even though I had not encouraged Graham, his attention gave me an emotional boost.

For the first few years after we moved, Jake and I would often drive back to town to visit Andy. Other times, he would arrive on our doorstep, an overnight bag in his hand and a wide smile on his face.

'Any nearer to starting your own business?' I often asked hopefully in the first couple of years, for I still felt disappointment that he had not pursued his interest in electronics and computers. But after a while I gave up mentioning this when I realised these questions embarrassed him. His visits gradually petered out, as did the invites for us to join him in town. He told us he had met a girl, Tracey. Of course, I wanted to meet her, but he always came up with some excuse whenever I mentioned it. Must be love, I suppose, was all I thought then.

We did speak every week on the phone but that didn't stop me from feeling concern that he was beginning to distance himself from us. A concern I pushed aside for it came at a time when I was beginning to feel dissatisfied with Jake's and my relationship.

Another year went by and then another, before I finally plucked up enough courage to leave him. Not that I didn't love him, it was more because I did. Although he was tearful when I told him, there was also a sense of relief at my decision, I think. I decided to stay in the village while I sorted out future plans – I had already found a room there. Meanwhile, I just kept my fingers crossed, hoping Tracey was the right one and was making my brother happy, for I always felt that under those boyish smiles and amusing stories was a troubled man.

Graham, on discovering that I had moved out, found where I was staying and came round to ask me out; he too had broken up with his partner some time ago and was now free. I said no to begin with, but after two or three visits from him, I gave in. Several dates followed, where he treated me as though I was a delicate piece of porcelain. He kept telling me how beautiful I was and how he could not believe his luck.

Looking back, if I had got to know him a little better, I would never have decided to move in with him so quickly. I can still hardly believe that it only took him a couple of months to persuade me. So, why did I? At twenty-nine he was the first man with whom I willingly had sex. It was something that he was very good at. I have to admit that was the main reason I thought I had fallen in love. If I had been a woman who had had flings like many of my friends before settling down, I might have known that late-awakened lust is not the same thing as love. Love is about caring, wanting the important person in one's life to be happy. It's not about being possessive and domineering, which Graham was to an obsessive degree. Oh, at first, I was flattered when he suggested which clothes he wanted me to wear and how he liked my hair tied back when we were out. He kept saying I did not need make-up, my skin was good enough. Once he got his own way on my appearance, he began to criticise my friends then told me he was not happy with my going out with them – he was worried that we might have too much to drink. And stupid me, I gave in. Once he saw he had gained some control, he upped the stakes. One little trick was not to give me the correct time of when we were going out. Then, just as I was pulling on my clothes, he would shout up the stairs, asking what was keeping me.

'You said eight,' I would say, looking at my watch.

'No, seven thirty,' would be his reply.

On the journey, he would sound almost kindly when he began to tell me he was concerned about my memory, though most of the time when he spoke to me there was an undercurrent of exasperation in his voice. It took me two years before I woke up to what kind of man he really was: a control freak who tried to make me feel inadequate. He criticised everything I did, tried to isolate me from my friends and accused me of sleeping with every man under eighty he saw me talking to. Worse, he tried to make me believe I was mentally unstable and that only he, who loved me despite all my inadequacies, could tolerate me.

When I faced up to what was really going on in that relationship, I threw everything into a suitcase, took Jed and made my escape. Time for a change, I decided. I knew I would have to move back to Hull.

Andy was the one I rang.

'Don't say any more now,' he said when I began to pour my heart out, 'just get on that train. I'll meet you. You can stay at my flat as long as you like. You can meet Tracey, I know you two will get on.'

He had told me a little about her on the phone. She was half-Chinese, came from a broken family, her mother had committed suicide, but she was doing alright now. He was clearly besotted and if Tracey was making my brother happy, I wanted to be friends with her.

At the station he wrapped his arms around me, said how pleased he was to see me, confessed that he had never liked Graham and asked if there was anything he could do to help.

'No, I just want to get Jed and me settled, then plan what I'm going to do next, but first, I really need to get a job,' I told him.

'We can talk about that later,' was his only comment. After patting Jed's upturned head, he picked up my suitcase and led me to his rather dilapidated old car. 'Motor's good, though, haven't lost the knack,' he told me as the engine roared into life.

I had noticed when he hugged me that my brother had lost a lot of weight. As he drove, I kept glancing at his profile: his cheekbones appeared sharp as razor blades and his face was so pale, it was almost ashen.

'Are you alright?' I asked.

'Yes, why?'

And I recognised the defensive tone that informed me whatever was wrong with him, he had no intention of confiding in me.

'Oh, I just thought you looked a bit pale, thinner too,' was all I said.

'City life, Sis, that's all.'

*

I felt a massive relief when Andy pulled up outside his flat. At last I could spend some time with my brother, catch up on our lives – all without Graham listening to every word and interrupting whenever he could.

For some reason, I hadn't expected Tracey to be there. It was she who, hearing the car pull up, opened the door to us. I saw a little wisp of a girl, who, with her fair hair tied into plaits and her round face devoid of make-up, looked, at first glance, little more than a child. A second glance though showed both the lines around her eyes and their hardness. While Andy in his blue jeans and leather jacket looked immaculate, there was something almost grubby about her appearance. She was undeniably pretty, but there was an air of remoteness about her too.

'Right,' she said once we were inside, 'you'll be happy, I'm sure, to have some peace. The settee makes into a bed and I've put bedding behind it. I'm going out with a friend tonight to leave you two alone.'

She smiled, but I was not fooled. Right from the start, I felt that she had no intention of us being friends. I noticed the yellow stains on her fingers and the dirt beneath her nails; her grubbiness was certainly not caused by housework, for the flat appeared none too clean either. What on earth did Andy see in her? Not that I asked him, I just thanked her instead.

Come on, Lynn, I told myself, she's trying. Don't judge her yet.

That evening, once Tracey had left, Andy and I went out to a local pub for a meal, downed a few beers and then returned to the flat, where we talked into the small hours. I did not ask where Tracey was, nor did he mention her absence. She arrived back mid-morning and made herself coffee before vanishing into the bedroom.

I spent the morning cleaning up as best I could. After the kitchen had some kind of order restored, I got Andy to drive me to the shops, where I picked up some groceries. Judging by the mountain of empty cartons I had thrown out, they lived on takeaways. Well, I didn't and nor should my brother – no wonder he looked pale and thin. I packed everything into the now-clean fridge and prepared lunch for the three of us.

Tracey appeared, a cloud of smoke drifting from her nostrils. She pushed the food around on her plate, lit up another cigarette while I was still eating and then asked me my plans for the future. Meaning, I thought, how long are you going to be staying?

I told her that there were two things I had to take care of: look for work and find a place to live, somewhere that was dog-friendly.

'Oh, there's no hurry, Sis,' Andy said. 'We like the idea of having you here, don't we, Tracey?'

'Yes, of course,' she answered, not that I believed for a moment that she meant it.

I knew the small talk between us was forced. Soon I began to feel it was because there was something she was hiding from me. The sharpness of her expression when she glanced sideways in my direction belied her superficial friendliness. Much as I wanted to spend time with my brother, I did not want to be around her any more than was absolutely necessary. I had money saved up, so I was not under pressure to find work, but also did not want my savings to be eaten up.

I had decided when I packed my bags that it was the very last time I was going to move out of a place I had looked on as home. Now it was time to become truly independent, which meant not falling into another bad relationship. I had an idea in my head of starting up a cleaning company; perhaps I could find another two or three people to work with me. Cleaning was something I was good at, as was cooking. To start with, I just needed to find a job and get a little more money in the bank though. I wanted to buy a decent car because having my own transport would be a step in the right direction.

Time to stop relying on others, I told myself firmly.

Hotel work, I decided, would be best. I would be able to live in and without household expenses, I could save quite a lot. Then I saw an ad in the local paper: a hotel in Gilberdyke, another small village just a thirty-mile drive from Hull, was advertising for staff. I applied, went for an interview and was given the job of assistant manager. I could also take Jed with me as long as there were no complaints from the guests. As soon as I knew my hours, I enrolled with the local driving school. Those lessons and Jed's food were my only real expenses. Three months later, I passed my test and was simply overjoyed.

When I held that driving test pass certificate, my first thought was that I was going to collect the car I had already paid off the deposit on, then drive to Hull and surprise my brother. I couldn't wait to see the expression on his face when he saw the secondhand Honda Civic I had bought. But I didn't want to ring – that would have killed the surprise element.

When I reached his flat, I pipped the horn, expecting to see his face appear at the window. Nothing happened. Must be out, I thought, then I saw Tracey walking up the road towards me.

'Hi,' I said, 'where's Andy? I thought I would pay him a visit.'

'You'd better come in,' was all she said, but by the expression on her face I knew two things: she was not pleased to see me and something was definitely wrong.

'So, where is he then?' I asked the moment I was perched on the edge of the stained settee. If I had thought the flat was messy before, since I had last visited it was much, much worse. Overflowing ashtrays, empty bottles and takeaway boxes were piled on the coffee table. The carpet had not seen a vacuum cleaner for a while, nor did I believe that the windows had once been opened to let in fresh air since I left. The place stank of grime and Tracey's unwashed body and clothes.

'Sorry, not had time to clear up. Wasn't expecting you,' was her half-hearted excuse. Not that I thought she would have bothered even if she had known. She lit a cigarette, inhaled deeply and looked at me through the plume of smoke that she released into the already polluted air.

'So, you want to know where your brother is. You haven't heard then?'

I wanted to scream, 'No, or why would I be asking, you stupid bitch?' But I just shook my head.

'He's in prison, isn't he? Caught dealing, the stupid bastard!'

'Dealing what?' I asked, hoping she was going to tell me it was dope, although I already knew that did not normally carry a prison sentence.

'Heroin,' she replied casually and my heart sank.

'Oh, no doubt you want to know why,' said Tracey, a small mocking smile on her face. 'He needs money, that's why.'

'But he works.'

'Is that what he told you? Well, he doesn't. He's on the social and they don't pay him enough for his habit, do they?'

With that last sentence she confirmed what I had expected to hear ever since she had said prison and dealing.

'You mean, my brother's a junkie?'

'Yes, has been for ages.'

And you are too, I thought.

'And who got him on it, Tracey?' I asked, my temper rising.

'His childhood, I expect. Who knows?'

Now I knew why Andy had looked so gaunt and pale. I also knew that I was sitting in the same room as the person who had got him addicted. It explained the hold she had over him. But those thoughts were best kept private, at least for the time being – I still needed more information.

'Is he in Hull?'

'Where else? Suppose you want to visit him. Feel free, I've no plans to go. Standing in a queue with all those other pathetic slags visiting their men is definitely not for me.'

As I glanced up at her sharp nose, thin lips and those dark eyes that gave nothing away, rage was building inside of me. She held my gaze for several long seconds. I knew she felt my contempt for her and I in turn felt her dislike of me. There was nothing more to say. I could have shouted insults at her, or done what my fingers were itching to do, pin her against the wall and thump her. But I had no intention of giving her the satisfaction of losing my cool.

'I don't suppose you know the visiting times?'

'No, you'll have to ring, won't you?'

She gave me another mocking smile and I bit my tongue, got up and left. On my way, I made the necessary phone calls and on my next free day from work, I went to visit my brother.

I queued up with the other visitors, was searched and then directed to where I had to go. By the time I sat in front of Andy, I felt there was a fresh layer of dirt clinging to my skin. Of course, there was part of me angry with him – drugs, apart from the odd joint, were something I was totally opposed to.

It was an anger that evaporated the moment I saw him. Separated by that glass partition, he was a shrunken version of the brother I had known. I could have cried then. Why hadn't I guessed the secret bond between those two? Everything had been there in front of me – his thinness, that pallor, the squalor he lived in and Tracey, with her dirty fingernails and furtive sideways glances. Of course, they had been hiding something: their addiction.

He told me that he had come off heroin. Well, of course he had no choice where he was. He was on prescribed methadone. And yes, I had heard of it. He kept saying how sorry he was. Sorry that he had let me down. I did not ask him who had got him started on it – I knew. All I could hope for was that he would turn away from Tracey when he was released. He said again that he was sorry he had taken drugs and I looked into his eyes.

'No, Andy, you didn't take drugs, *they* took you.'

He did not reply, just started muttering about our father: 'I never did enough, did I? Never stood up to that bastard, just wasn't man enough to stop him.'

'For heaven's sake, Andy, don't use that as a reason for your being in here! I'd like to know who planted those ideas in your head. We were children, what could you have done?'

Hearing the exasperation in my voice, he quietened down then. I saw tears form in his eyes when it was time for me to go. There was a lump in my throat too. I knew though that if I allowed myself to be tearful, it would do more harm than good – I had to be the stronger one. So, I bit my lip hard to keep the tears at bay, said my goodbyes and told him I would be back to visit on my next day off.

Once outside, I breathed the fresh air deep into my lungs gratefully. The prison had stifled me. What to do next, I asked myself. I had to be able to help my brother once he was released, protect him as well. I was only too aware that it was only a small percentage of people who managed to kick their habit, and the most important thing was that they really had to want to.

I visited every week and what were his most frequently asked questions? Had I seen Tracey? Was she alright and would I tell her that he was thinking of her? All of which made me want to scream. Not that I dared point out that she was part of the problem – he would not see it.

I planned to take him away for the weekend once he was released, a plan inevitably foiled by Tracey. It was she who arranged to meet him at the prison gate. Well, we were both there, but it was she he walked off with. Oh, I was invited to join them. But then he did not see, or did not want to, the animosity between us. As far as Andy was concerned, Tracey was his girlfriend and girlfriends must come first. His excuse for her not visiting was that she would have found it too upsetting.

If he objected to the squalor she was happy to live in, he never mentioned it.

I played the game of the understanding sister well – 'No, you two need to spend some time together' – and gave him a hug and told him I would see him soon.

I tried to get him to go to Narcotics Anonymous. He went once or twice then stopped. So, the heroin won, he went back on it. Not only that, he began to drink heavily as well.

Part Three
The Circle of Life

Chapter Thirty-One

Visiting Andy and worrying about him took up a lot of my time. I gave up the idea of forming my own small company and found another job that paid better. It was as a housekeeper for a couple who lived in a huge greystone manor house or 'The Hall' as it was called locally. My employers were easy-going and generous. I could live in or out, except when they were away on holiday, then they wanted someone resident. Also, dogs were welcome. There were plenty of grounds for Jed to run around in – I think he thought he was in heaven when I started working there.

It was when Andy told me that he and Tracey were having problems and were splitting that I decide to rent somewhere in the village and began looking for a place large enough for the two of us. I wanted to make him better, feed him healthy food and help him reduce his alcohol intake. There were local walks I planned to take him on – surely breathing in the fresh country air would be good for him? But before I signed the rental agreement, I made it clear to my brother that as long as he was going to Narcotics Anonymous again, he could move in with me. He agreed, both to that and to using methadone to try to keep his addiction under control.

After only a few days of us living together, it became obvious that Andy had just replaced one addiction with another. He did not even try to hide from me that he sipped alcohol all day long.

I had no idea where he was getting the money from. 'Fixing things,' he told me when I asked. But then I was supplying him with food, not that he ate much, and was paying all the household bills, so I suppose all his social security went to keep him in drink.

I wanted my beautiful brother back – the one who would sit with his arm around my shoulder, chatting away. The one who raced motorbikes on the railway tracks and bought me thoughtful gifts with the money he earned. There were few signs that this person was left: this brother was almost a stranger to me. There are some memories that take a lot of coaxing to bring to the front of our minds while others float clear and bright in the air in front of our eyes. A memory that kept coming back to me was of a time when we were in Scotland. We had been taken to the coast and Andy and I were hopping over the sand dunes, giggling away until one of our parents shouted out for us to stop. He took my hand and, joined together as one being, the two of us ran back to them. Now the adult Andy sat morosely on the sofa, staring into space at a past he was powerless to stop visiting.

About a year after Andy had moved in with me, my stepbrother Gavin introduced me to a friend of his, Steve. A tall man, with greying dark hair, he was a few years older than Gavin. The fact that his children, who he referred to as 'kids', were somewhere in their early twenties made me guess that he was late forties or even early fifties. He was in insurance, he said. 'Oh, not people's lives,' he added with a laugh, 'buildings.'

I liked him straight away. Not only was he caring towards Gavin, but he accepted Andy without comment. The word 'kind' sprang to mind when I noticed that. We became good friends fairly quickly. Gavin had already told me that Steve was separated from his wife. Although he could not live with her any longer, he still went to see her regularly to make sure she was alright.

It took a long time for Steve and me to progress from friends to lovers, but eventually we did. Maybe it was the way he accepted Andy that drew me to him, or it might have been that, being around twenty years older than me, he appeared to be reliable and safe. He explained that when he and his wife separated, he had taken a small flat in Hull, somewhere near his work and nice enough for the kids to visit. The couple of times I had suggested we had a night out in Hull though, he became evasive. He gave his children as an excuse and told me he never knew when they would drop in and it was still too soon for them to know about another woman in his life.

I believed him – I suppose we believe what we want to. He started staying with me two or three nights a week. After a year or so, I discovered I was pregnant and was overjoyed. He, on the other hand, was not: he wanted me to have a termination. My response was that if he did not want the baby, I would bring the child up myself and he could stay in Hull. I did not let him know that I had already spoken to my employers, who seemed pleased for me and said that I could bring the baby to work with me. This arrangement gave me the confidence to stand up to Steve.

He relented and told me it was just his age – he had two almost grown-up children and it was grandchildren he had been looking forward to, not more children of his own. He assured me not only would he help financially, he knew he would love the baby as soon as she or he arrived.

*

For the next couple of months, I tried desperately to help get Andy off the booze.

'I don't want my baby born into a home with a bad atmosphere,' I told him. 'You're going to be an uncle and uncles are expected to set a good example.'

He went to the doctor, who prescribed sedatives and anti-booze pills. For a couple of weeks, he sobered up. Of course, each time that happened I prayed it would last. But it didn't and at the end of two weeks, he was back on the booze again and the pills remained untouched. Then he started disappearing for the odd night.

I knew before he told me that he was seeing Tracey again – 'She's asked if she can visit us here, wants us all to be friends,' he told me nonchalantly. She's the last person I want in my home, I felt like saying, and 'friends' was just not going to happen. I didn't, though – I was scared that if I refused, he would disappear completely. So, I gave in. No smoking in the house was one rule I made and she was not to bring any drink in either.

It did not take me long to work out what Tracey's visit was about. I had a washing machine, a bathroom and a fridge full of food – all of which she helped herself to without any offer to contribute.

While I waited for my baby to be born, I watched the Andy I had known gradually disappear. I was convinced by his appearance that it was not only alcohol that was causing the changes in him. His hair had thinned and was streaked with grey, his teeth blackened until the front ones dropped out. Deep down, I guessed that he was back on drugs and there was nothing left for me to do. Drink did not turn teeth rotten and make them drop out. Nor, I thought, did heroin as far as I knew, but I couldn't bring myself to face up to what it might be. I had to concentrate on my growing baby, I told myself, though I wondered just how I was going to cope if things got any worse with my brother. I was certain the only liquids he took came from a bottle and not one that contained sparkling water. At least most of the time he was able to hold it well. He rarely appeared drunk, but I knew why that was: his body had become completely alcohol-dependent. The odd time he was clearly the worse for wear I did not like him. He reminded me of another man who was an unpleasant drunk: our father.

When I pointed this out, Andy flew into a rage. A tirade of spite was unleashed from his lips as he paced up and down for half an hour, shouting out what he wanted to do to our father.

'I'm going to report him to the police,' he yelled. 'Time I stood up to him, made him suffer. Where's the phone? I've got his number, I'm going to tell him myself what I'm going to do.'

I was too frightened by that angry Andy to ask how he had the number. I had not had any contact with our father since he got rid of our dog, Judy. I found out later that Michelle's mother, Maggie, had it because he rang her occasionally to check how we were so Andy must have wheedled it out of her. I tried to calm him and said we had to put it all behind us, but he refused to listen.

'Don't be so bloody soft, Lynn! I'm doing it.'

He snatched up the phone and dialled. Of course, I could not hear what was being said at the other end of the line, but I could hear my brother repeat the threats he had been spouting. His voice went quiet a couple of times; he was listening and whatever he was hearing pleased him. After about twenty minutes, he replaced the phone on the receiver and turned to me with a triumphant smile I did not like one bit.

'That's sorted him at last. He was begging me not to do it, told me he knew he had been a bad father and he was sorry. Well, I refused to listen. He can sit there quaking with fear, let him know what it feels like. Every knock on his door will send him into a panic and it serves him right. Not that I expect he gets many visitors. Do you know where he is, Lynn?'

'Scotland somewhere,' I said, for I had been told by Maggie that he had returned there.

'Yes, but you don't know where he's living, do you?'

I shook my head.

'In sheltered accommodation for the elderly. God, he's fallen alright! And do you know what else he told me? No, of course you don't. He's got prostate cancer. Advanced, he says.'

'Enough, Andy, I've heard enough,' I told him.

It was that phone call that motivated me to contact my father. Whatever he had done, I could not bear the thought of him ending his life being constantly afraid. If there was one thing I had learnt it was that hate turns into a weapon that only attacks the person who feels it. I only had to look at my brother to see what it had done to him. His shame at not being able to look after me when we were young had caused all that hatred. Over the years it had eaten its way inside, consuming his mind and body until only a shell remained.

At that time Andy had little energy to even go out to get booze, let alone anything else, so I knew there was no chance of him carrying out his threat. But our father was not to know that. I could not bring myself to be pleased that he was scared and alone, waiting for death and the police to come. Maybe I shouldn't have cared, but I did. After all, I was still his daughter and now I was expecting a child of my own. Once Andy had shuffled off to bed, I pressed the recall button and waited for the line to connect.

'Hello Dad, it's Lynn,' I said and heard him gasp. He must have thought that I was going to confirm Andy's threats. I told him not to worry: Andy was not going to the police, I would not let him.

He broke down on hearing those words. I could hear him choking back sobs. Why, I thought, he's become a sad old man, just as Andy predicted.

'Thank you, oh, thank you, Lynn,' he managed to get out.

By Christmas 2010, I was nearly four months pregnant. My baby bulge was already showing. I replaced my jeans with leggings and searched the charity shops for outsized shirts and jumpers that my bump and I could grow into. That combination, I decided, was more flattering to me than a baggy maternity dress. A thermal vest underneath and I was warm, both inside and out. I was so looking forward to meeting that little person growing inside me.

Steve had spent Christmas Eve with both Andy and me, where Christmas presents and cards were exchanged. I received perfume, body lotion and scented candles. I gave them colourful woollen scarves. Steve had already told me he was spending both Christmas and Boxing Day with his 'kids', as he insisted on calling his two adult children, and left late that evening. After giving me a kiss on the way out, he said he wished he didn't have to go, but still, we would only be apart for two days.

The question that had been running through my head ever since he had informed me of his plans was why, with a baby on the way – which would, after all, be his two children's half-brother or sister, Steve had still not introduced me to them. A question I still did not ask.

I had decorated the tree, placed cards around all the free surfaces and made the room look as cheerful as possible. Michelle and her parents were coming for Christmas lunch. I was so happy that for once I could entertain them. Andy was in one of his sober spells and apart from not having Steve with me, it was going to be a perfect day. And it was. Andy remained sober, helped with everything and the whole day felt as Christmas should, a traditional day with friends and family.

True to his word, Steve, all smiles and full of goodwill, arrived back two days later. He took me in his arms and said how much he had missed me. Not enough though to have stopped him having made arrangements to see in the New Year with the 'kids'. I was more than disappointed when he said that he could not wriggle out of the party they had arranged and of course, he had to be there. He kept repeating he would much rather be with me and asked if I understood. 'No, I don't,' would have been the truthful answer, but I just smiled and said I did.

Once the sound of his car leaving could be heard, Andy asked me to join him and Tracey for the evening. 'You can stay over,' he suggested. 'Don't want to think of you being here on your own, Sis, your last New Year without a child.' It was an invitation I declined. While I would have liked to be with my brother, I had no wish to spend any time with Tracey, let alone step over the threshold of her filthy flat. Not that I said that. Instead, I reassured him that I was happy to be on my own and that I would watch the festivities on television.

'Well then, see you next year,' he said with a grin as he went out.

I felt a wave of loneliness: 'Wish you were here already,' I told my bump, cradling its girth.

It was while I was settling down in front of the TV with a mug of hot chocolate that the phone rang.

It'll be Steve, I thought happily, as I picked it up. But it wasn't. It was someone quite different: his wife. She had found my Christmas card and read what I had written – 'All my love Lynn', followed by a row of kisses. As she spoke, or rather screamed abuse down the phone, I knew why he had been staying away. I heard her shouting that I was a good-for-nothing slut and to stay away from her husband if I knew what was good for me. Before I could get any words out to defend myself, she swore at me again and rang off.

I wanted to throw everything of Steve's out of the house, get in my car and drive into Hull and confront him. I was having his baby, for Christ's sake. Don't you remember that article you read about how a mother's anxiety can be transferred to the baby while it's in the womb? I told myself instead. So, calm down, Lynn and think about the tiny person who relies on you. I stroked my bulge and whispered to it soothingly.

'Everything going to be alright, baby,' I kept repeating.

But was it?

*

The following morning, Steve burst through the door, both angry and worried. Excuses fell from his lips almost as soon as he arrived. He swore his wife had lied, that he only spent time at his house to make sure she was alright and to meet up with his children.

'Grown-up children who are old enough to know about parents separating?' I pointed out.

He agreed and said they knew now that he had left the marital home. 'I'm going to stay with you, Lynn,' he assured me, 'you and our baby.'

Did I believe him? No. I wanted to, more for the baby's sake than my own, but I didn't. Although that still did not stop me from allowing him to stay.

'Should've chucked the bastard straight out,' Andy told me indignantly when he heard. And of course, for once, my brother was right. But then I'm not the only person to have postponed the inevitable.

For the next three months Steve divided his time between two homes. There were always excuses, ones I hardly ever believed. I might have wanted him to remain with me and wanted to believe that everything would be alright once our baby was born and that she – and yes, I had been told I was going to have a girl – would have two loving parents and a sober uncle. That hope did not stop me being aware that whatever excuse he made, Steve was still spending time with his wife. Any more than it stopped me knowing that Andy was now seriously back on drugs.

It was when I was seven months pregnant that I finally faced up to these facts and that my wishes for them to be dealt with were unlikely to ever come true. I suddenly felt I needed to be closer to my friends; I could not bring up Kate, as I had already named her, so far apart from help being just a phone call away, so I took a decision that I was going to move back to where my roots were: Hessle. That was where the friends I had grown up with were – Kate was going to need more people in her life than just me.

In March, with Maggie's help, I found a house that I thought would be perfect for us all. There was plenty of room for three adults and a baby. Kate came a month before she was expected. I woke in the middle of the night to a damp bed and a worried man.

Steve had made it clear from the moment he knew I was pregnant that he would not be with me for the birth. He would most probably faint was his excuse. I had asked Michelle to be there and she had said yes, but she was away on a work-related course so I got Steve to phone another friend, Heidi, while I gathered up the items I needed – it had been too early to pack a bag. Then it was a race to get to the hospital. A kiss was bestowed on my head before Steve turned and left me there. It was Heidi who sat holding my hand, wiping the sweat from my forehead and breathing with me.

After a gruelling eleven-hour labour and two failed epidurals, the midwife told me that they would have to take the baby out by caesarean. 'Is she alright?' I kept asking, until I was in the theatre and counting slowly backwards.

I came round later in the recovery room, dreading the worst, but no, there was a picture of my little girl, with lots of curly black hair and a tiny little face. Kate, the light of my life, had come into the world. She weighed just three pounds and twelve ounces.

The doctor explained that we would both have to stay in for a week. My baby had to reach four pounds before she could leave and I had to recover from the caesarean operation.

Steve came to visit and told me Kate was a beautiful baby but I felt a distance between us. The moment Heidi came back into the room, it was as though he breathed a sigh of relief before making a hasty retreat – a retreat I almost welcomed. I could not bring myself to forgive him for not being by my side when I brought our daughter into the world.

'Not ours, but mine,' I kept telling myself.

Eleven hours of pain and pushing, and it was worth every painful second. But that did not wipe out the fact that Steve had not been there when I needed him. For Katy's sake I said nothing – I wanted her to have a father. At least he picked us up on the day the doctor said we were ready to go home. As we left the hospital, I held my precious bundle in my arms while he carried my case. Once I reached home, both Andy and Heidi would be waiting for me. I had asked them to put off any other visitors – I needed time to rest a little and to get to know my daughter.

As we drove to the house, I could feel Steve's unease.

'I need to talk to you, Lynn,' he said, before adding 'privately' after a long pause.

I knew what it was he wanted to say.

'You can tell me in the car, Steve. Although I think I can probably guess,' I said.

Oh, he said he was sorry and he hadn't meant to hurt anyone; none of this was his fault, of course. It was just that Pam, his wife, could not cope without him. She had threatened suicide. He said that I was strong, I would be alright without him. He had no other choice than to stay with her, did he?

I interrupted this barrage of self-pitying excuses: 'Steve, just get it over with, get all your stuff and go!' I snapped.

'I'll come by and see her every day,' he told me. 'You'll let me do that, won't you?'

What choice did I have? He was Kate's father, so I agreed. For eight days he kept his promise. After that, it was only once or twice a week until his visits dwindled. Now he still sees her occasionally. It's a secret, though – his wife must never find out. Well, it's not a new story, is it? It was just a new one for me.

He was right, though: I could manage without him. In fact, I hardly missed him, I was so enraptured with my child.

I have only one word to describe what my early weeks were like when I got to know my daughter: joyful. I watched her feeding as I held her, rubbed her back to wind her and listened to that tiny burp telling me she was full. When I lifted her up a little higher to stare into her face, her lashes lifted and in her navy eyes, I was sure even then I could see her trust in me.

In the evenings, I followed the routine that the health visitor had recommended: bath, feed, place in cot, turn on baby monitor. Sometimes this deserted me. This is not love, I thought. Instead, I placed her in the crook of my arm, her head wedged beneath my chin, and inhaled her perfume of new skin, baby soap and talcum as I lay drowsy with contentment on the settee.

When friends visited, they too billed and cooed over her. 'Can I hold her, just for a minute?' was the most frequently asked question. And smilingly, I would pass her over.

By the time she was a month old and had filled out a little they kept teasing me, 'She looks just like you, Lynn,' or 'I can see who she takes after.' She looks like herself, I thought. I failed to see my younger face was hidden beneath those rosy apple cheeks.

I find it hard to believe now that it has been eight years since I brought Katy home. Those years since she was born have been both good ones and bad. But then that's life, isn't it?

At first the joy inside me that Katy gave me made me more tolerant. I wanted everyone to feel as I felt. Once I had contacted my father again, he started ringing me. He asked me to visit him – he would come down himself, but he understood that he would not be welcomed by his son. Nor, I wanted to say, by me. I was alright with his phone calls but I was not yet ready to meet him again.

It was after Katy was born that I agreed. He had cried on the phone when I told him about her, he begged me to let him see his grandchild. Hearing him sob made me relent so I packed her into the baby seat, filled the back of the car with everything a baby might need for forty-eight hours and drove to Scotland.

My father had invited me to stay in the guest room of the sheltered housing block he was in – he would just have to book one and he'd pay, he said. It was an invitation to which I said a firm no: 'I'm staying at a B&B,' I told him. He did not argue for he understood the reason behind my refusal.

I had expected him to appear frail – his voice on the phone indicated this was most likely to be the case – but when I met him, I was shocked by the change in him. In the years since I had stood on his doorstep and been told that he had got rid of my dog, he had aged more than I would have believed possible.

His once-thick hair had thinned, there was a faint silvery fuzz on his jaw and his fingers my mother once said were so elegant and I only remembered as being hard and brutal shook when he held even a cup of tea. He was, as he had sounded on the phone, an unthreatening, ill, old man. He was lonely, he told me. I felt like saying there had never been a need for him to be, it was the path he had chosen that had resulted in his isolation.

Even after everything he had done to the child I had once been, I had tried to accept him but he had thrown all of that back in my face when he sold our home and got rid of the dog I had loved so much. Not that I could bring myself to say that, or to tell him there are punishments for people who act like he had and the way he had to live out the rest of his life was it.

Why had I gone? That's a question more than one person has asked me, one I still do not have the full answer to. Was it so some of my questions could be answered? To have the last word perhaps or tell him what a monster he had been? Or was it really pity that made me make that journey? Maybe it was a mixture of all three.

He told me he had found religion, repented, and that he was so sorry for what he had done. But he made no excuses, at least not then.

I spent the day with him.

He asked if I forgave him.

So, did I?

I felt like saying that it was not for me to forgive him his sins. I might not have felt hatred any longer, but forgiveness was another matter entirely.

'You're my father,' I said, 'let's just leave it at that.'

I drove back the next day. As I drove, I felt lighter for that chapter had finally reached its end, or so I thought.

When Katy was only a few months old, I lost my grandmother. I was just pleased that she had lived long enough to meet my daughter. Two years later, in 2012, when Katy was not much more than a toddler, I lost two close friends. One of them was Michelle's mother Maggie, who succumbed to breast cancer. The other, a man I had known since he was a boy, died in a car accident. Two funerals of people I had loved in one year.

A little later, my brother was rushed into hospital. I suspected when I rang for the ambulance that there would shortly be a third burial to attend. Although he had weaned himself off the booze with medication, he was still far from well. He was admitted to hospital with chronic heart failure and spent three weeks there before he was finally allowed home with lots of different medication that he would have to take for the rest of his life. While he'd been in hospital, I'd thoroughly cleaned and tidied his room. Not a job I enjoyed – it was dirty and foul-smelling. After opening the windows to allow some air in, I pulled on rubber gloves and cleaned everywhere I could. I stripped the bed, picked up every single article of clothing and threw it in the washing machine.

When I brought him home from the hospital, Andy was so weak I wondered how I was going to cope with his care as well as Katy's. That worry was soon replaced by another: Tracey, who had lost every scrap of prettiness she once had and was almost as dirty as Andy's room, had begun visiting. I could not have stopped him going to her, but now he was too weak, I was expected to tolerate her coming into my home.

As soon as he felt he was on the road to recovery and a little colour returned to his face, he started drinking again. If that was not the final straw, the smell of dope leaking out from under his door was.

'No,' I told Tracey, 'I have a child.'

'No,' I said to Andy, 'this no longer works.'

It was my final statement concerning our living arrangement.

I went flat and house hunting again. This time I found a two-bedroomed cottage for myself and a small flat for Andy. I got him moved in and then sighed with relief. It was just Katy and me now and a safe environment was essential, something I was determined for her to have.

Katy loved her new home, played happily in the garden and in 2014, she began nursery school.

Chapter Thirty-Two

I had just returned from taking Katy to nursery school when my doorbell rang. I opened the door and to my astonishment, it was my father, who had grown much frailer since I visited him, standing on the doorstep.

'What on earth are you doing here?' I asked, more than a little apprehensive.

'A friend gave me a lift,' he said quickly, 'we've brought you some family things that I thought you would want. Can I come in?'

He beckoned to his friend, who was sitting in the car. He carried over a couple of large boxes and asked my father what time he should pick him up.

'I have to leave in an hour,' I told him firmly, determined there was a limited time in place for this unwanted visit. Admittedly, I did not have to leave nearly so soon, but I did not want my father to begin to feel too comfortable and decide to spend the whole day with me.

'Lynn, there is something I have to tell you,' he said.

'As soon as I have made us both some tea,' I told him, walking into the kitchen with him trailing behind me.

'It will help you understand everything. I have not got long to go now, I know that, and I don't want to leave this world with all my secrets,' he continued.

By that, I guessed he wanted to bring up my childhood and make some sort of excuse for his actions. An excuse I did not wish to hear. He might want to unburden his conscience if he really was dying, I supposed, although I doubted his excuses would be given much credence by me or wherever he was going once he finally left this world.

Taking our tea through to the lounge, I avoided the sofa and indicated a chair to him while I chose the other one.

'Lynn, I honestly believed it was what fathers did,' he announced calmly.

I'm sure my knuckles whitened as I gripped the edge of the armchair so hard to keep myself from jumping up in anger. Shocked by that statement, I forced myself not to respond, but to stay silent, and waited for him to speak.

'You must want to know why, Lynn?'

No, I absolutely didn't. I already guessed whatever he had to say was not something I wished to hear.

'My own father told me that when he first came into my room when I was a boy. He told me that again when he beat me.'

'Grandpa?' I whispered.

'Who else?'

Thinking of the man I had loved so much in these terms made me feel sick – sick and totally betrayed. An unwanted picture squirmed its way into my head, a bewildered child being told a lie. Not a little lie but a huge one I had so wanted to believe. It was the night my grandfather came into my room and did his best to convince me that a nightmare had caused me to fall out of bed: 'You hit your head,' he told me even though that had not been the part of me that was hurting. I knew I had seen blood

— blood that came from between my legs. He had given me a drink to make me feel better. And when I awoke, my pyjamas and bedding were clean. 'You had a nightmare,' he told me again. And now I knew the truth: my father had raped me, hurt me badly, and my grandfather had known and been complicit in inventing the lies.

'He covered up for you the time you hurt me, didn't he?' I said, angry with myself for not being able to shout out the real word I should have used in that sentence: rape. 'You went to him and asked him to help, didn't you? He must have put something in my drink to make me sleep and once I was unconscious, you two cleaned me up and changed both me and the bedding. That's what happened, isn't it?'

'Yes. I'm so sorry, Lynn.'

Sorry isn't good enough, I wanted to say, along with telling him to go and get out of my house forever. The only thing that stopped those words being uttered was that part of me wanted to hear what else he had to say. Though the other part wished he had never come and just left me with some of my illusions.

As I sat there, head bowed and my hands clenched in my lap, another memory slid into view: my grandfather telling me a story about when his mother became pregnant and how the man who was his biological father fled. The man she married was therefore not the father of her eldest son. Then me asking him if his stepfather had been good to him and his curt one-word answer 'no,' before he changed the subject.

'He was abused by his stepfather as well, wasn't he? And also told that was what fathers did.'

'Yes, Lynn, he was.'

'But their mothers, those men's wives, surely they knew?'

'The men never wanted them to know that and their wives hid their knowledge well. Perhaps they hid it from themselves as well. You see, Lynn, if they had admitted that they knew what their husbands were doing, they would have had to make a choice, wouldn't they? Either their men or their children.'

'And if they chose the first, they would have been enablers. So, what you are saying, Dad, is that by not being able to face the truth, they kept silent?'

He nodded.

So, was my father telling me something about my own mother? I suspect that he was. I could not bring myself to ask him anything more. My thoughts in turmoil, I heard the sound of a car hooting outside, signalling the hour was up. I heard him telling me again, as though his visit was a perfectly normal social one, that there were things in the boxes he thought I would like to have.

It was not until he had left the house that I thought of all the questions I could have asked, but then, didn't I really now know the answers?

I watched out of the window as he climbed into his friend's car stiffly. He smiled up at me and waved before closing the door. I remained standing there long after they had reached the end of the street and disappeared from view.

That was the last time I saw my father.

He died in the spring of the following year. I organised his funeral. It took place in Scotland, where he had asked to be buried. Andy came with me, but Gavin refused. There was only a handful of mourners, a few of the people who had lived near him and his carers.

The remainder of 2014 was uneventful although it was evident that Andy was getting ill more and more often. He just drank all the time, barely ate and was literally skin and bone. I tried to get him help, but it seemed he no longer wanted to fight his addictions and I suspected as he still saw Tracey, there would also be hard drugs involved.

In September, my little girl started school. Every mother knows what that first day is like. I missed her, but she, on the other hand, made new friends and told me she just loved it.

Early in 2015, I took Katy on holiday to Wales. The devastating phone call came while I was there.

My brother had died some time the previous evening. It was Tracey who found him, still sitting in his chair. While the death certificate stated he had died from kidney failure, I knew what really killed him: it was as a result of three generations of women choosing to remain silent and therefore failing their children. When Andy eventually came to know who the father he had placed on such a pedestal really was, something inside him changed. It took away his trust and over the years ate away at his very being. He was not strong enough to deal with the disillusionment. It was as though losing the love he had felt for his father left an aching hole inside him that he was incapable of filling.

And so, I had another funeral to arrange and another flat to clear out. I still have boxes of things brought from Andy's that I haven't been able to touch yet.

I arranged to have my brother cremated. Gavin, Michelle, Steve and Matt and a few close friends came. We scattered his ashes in a place we nicknamed 'Little Switzerland' – it has cliffs, woods and ponds, and when we were kids, it was his favourite place to go for picnics.

'At least you are free of your demons now, Andy,' I whispered as the gentle breeze carried away his ashes. I imagined I felt him there; a caress stroked my cheek and I heard his voice murmuring, 'You were always the strong one, Lynn, you'll be alright.'

Looking up, I saw a blue streak rising high in the sky.

'Goodbye, Andy,' I murmured to it.

My life moves on quietly now. On doctor's advice I gave up my housekeeping business, which I had eventually started a year earlier. He explained that after everything I had gone through, he felt I needed a peaceful few months and arranged for me to have grief counselling. Over time I have come to terms with the needless death of my brother. The counsellor and I inevitably touched on other factors and we worked through all the issues of my childhood too.

It was then that I decided to brush up my computer skills and enroll on a course. Katy found it amusing that we were, as she thought, both going to school. Gavin helped by collecting her when my hours were later than hers. In their time together, he was happy to find that his niece had inherited his love of painting. The two of them can sit together for hours, looking at art on the internet. In time I hope they will have a close bond, for he is after all her only uncle now.

Halfway through my course, I decided what I wanted to do once my studies were finished. A few weeks ago, I applied for the job I wanted and was given it. I'm now helping to teach young autistic adults, aged sixteen to twenty-five. Not just how to use computers, but other activities too – baking, gardening, enjoying walks, swimming and going on pub/cafe trips. When Gavin is free, he occasionally teaches an art class and loves it.

Some of my colleagues work with young people who are physically disabled, others with those who are classed as having special needs. All of us have the same goal: to show them how to live life to the full, to become independent and take pride in their achievements.

Epilogue

2019

It has been five years since I saw my father for the last time, five years since I opened those boxes, and five years since I learnt the secrets of not just one family but three – secrets that I never want my daughter to share. And now? My mind is no longer troubled. Discovering those albums not only helped put my memories in order, it helped me deal with them.

Yes, I know that I'm settled now. I also have good friends, a brother whom I have become very close to and a job that completely fulfils me. My daughter is doing amazingly well at school; she's a happy, well-adjusted child and brings me joy each and every day. She still sees her father every now and again, though he has still not told his wife about her. Katy and I are busy making another video, one that shows her growing from bump to the present day.

So, do I want to find another partner? Intent on matchmaking, friends often ask me that. 'Well, one control freak and one married lover who lied have put me off a little,' I tell them with a wry laugh. I do not mention my first love – Jake – who rolled back into my life when he heard of Andy's death.

I brushed aside his apologies before he introduced me to his new partner, David.

'Well, that explains a few things, Jake,' was all I said, giving them both hugs.

And it did.

The answer to my friends' question then is that maybe one day I will find the right person but my happiness will not rely on that: it will rely on me and who I am. And yes, I am happy and contented.

What more could anyone ask for?

Acknowledgements

I would like to thank my best friends, Heidi Hawkins and Jon Seth, for their unconditional friendship and support over the years. Also, Toni Maguire for her friendship and dedication. And a big thank you to Caroline, who I hear spent hours helping to shape my story.

Toni Maguire

One woman who found the courage to share her story
inspired others to find their voice

Toni Maguire has published two bestselling books that covered
her own story of her childhood abuse and finding a way of
moving on from her past, *Don't Tell Mummy* and *When Daddy
Comes Home*. Her success encouraged others who had kept
their childhood secrets hidden to approach her and share their
stories. She has so far co-written seven memoirs and sold over
1.5 million books worldwide. To find out more about Toni and
her story visit www.tonimaguire.co.uk

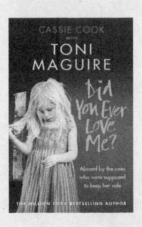

They Stole My Innocence

*The shocking true story of a young girl abused in
one of the most notorious care homes*

Five-year-old Madeleine was living a daily nightmare. In a
dark, grey building in Jersey, she was just another orphan,
defenceless and alone. Unbeknownst to the outside world,
the care home manager was using her like she was his toy. And,
worse still, the home was selling the children to men
who would inflict on them the worst possible abuse.

This is Madeleine's heartbreaking story and
her fight to survive.

ISBN 9781785033513

Order direct from www.penguin.co.uk

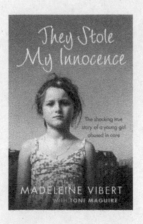